CONQUERING STRONGHOLDS

30-DAY BATTLE PLAN FOR WALKING IN PURITY

DR. SCOTT SILVERII

To every man who has taken the time and listened to, looked at and lifted up another man for no other reason than it was the right thing to do; I dedicate this book to you.

To access the free website Conquering Strongholds video course, visit:
https://www.fivestonespress.org/conquering

WHEN I WAS A CHILD

"When I was a child, I talked like a child, I thought like a child, I reasoned like a child. When I became a man, I put the ways of childhood behind me."

— GOD (1 CORINTHIANS 13:11)

CONTENTS

All Scripture quotations, unless otherwise indicated, are taken from the New American Standard Bible, ©1960, 1962, 1963, 1968, 1971, 1972, 1973, 1975, 1977, 1995 by The Lockman Foundation. Used by permission.

Other versions used are:

KJV—King James Version. Authorized King James Version.

NIV—Scripture taken from the Holy Bible, New International Version®. Copyright © 1973, 1978, 1984 by International Bible Society. Used by permission of Zondervan Publishing House. All rights reserved.

First Edition

Publisher: Five Stones Press, Dallas, Texas

For quantity sales, textbooks, and orders by trade bookstores or wholesalers contact Five Stones Press at publish@fivestonespress.net

Five Stones Press is owned and operated by Five Stones Church, a nonprofit 501c3 religious organization. Press name and logo are trademarked. Contact publisher for use.

Dr. Scott Silverii's website is scottsilverii.com

Printed in the United States of America

INTRODUCTION

I get it.

We're men, and part of who we are is to run and gun until we're out of ammo or just plain out of luck. So then what are we to do? We do the best we can. But wide open and unfocused isn't the best we can be. Sexual sin is killing us, and we're too busy high-fiv'n each other to realize it. Until we're out of ammo and out of luck.

My goal is to straight-talk you into an understanding of just how dangerous the consequences of sexual sin are. As men we grow up in a culture of promiscuity where sexual conquest is our rite of passage. The problem is, we aren't mentored in truth or reality. Instead of walking in the light with our heads held high, we're preoccupied with getting busted for coloring outside of the lines. Notice I'm saying "we," because this is our challenge and our chance to overcome. Also, we men are stronger together.

The reality is that there are severe consequences for living a life driven by and dependent upon sex as the platform upon which we base who we are as men.

I want to show you that freedom is yours through Christ. Breaking the chains of bondage can be tough, but not impossible. We're going to talk like men, and focus on key terms like endurance, surrender, submission, forgiveness, restoration and renewal that will become vital in gaining your freedom and restoring your life.

You'll soon know that although I'm not going to pull punches with you, I have a heart for Jesus. Some men may think that makes me soft, but I can assure you that there is nothing weak about Christ, the mighty King of kings.

God created us in His image and improving that image of you is a gift God gave. Living your life like the warrior that you were created to be is going to change your life and show the giver of the gift how we feel about Him.

But I discipline my body and keep it under control, lest after preaching to others I myself should be disqualified.
   1 Corinthians 9:27

Let's do this,
Scott

To access the free website Conquering Strongholds video course, visit: https://www.fivestonespress.org/conquering

DAY 1

FACING THE FACTS

It is actually reported that there is sexual immorality among you,
and of a kind that is not tolerated even among pagans, for a man
has his father's wife.
    1 Corinthians 5:1

———

Are you shackled down by the oppression of sexual sin? One of the great lies of sexual bondage is that it's a victimless act. We tell ourselves that the physical sex is consensual, the fantasy sex is subscribed to or free on websites, and the masturbation is done solo. So how in the world is acting out sexually going to hurt anyone?

I'll give credit where credit is due. Satan is masterful at his controlling deception. Sex is a powerful tool. Satan knows this and uses it against us every moment of every day. In media imaging, movies and magazines, in our own minds and almost everywhere we look, from the checkout girl's cleavage hinting beneath her uniform shirt to the ads that clutter your social media viewing.

The reality is, like the apostle Paul said above, your sexual activity is more widely known than you'd expect. Obviously, no matter how dark your room is, God knows your heart, but the reality is, you are not acting alone or undetected. You are betrayed by your thoughts and actions. People you trust your deviance to are also suffering as you are. There is no honor among sexual sinners, and it is not a victimless act. This is what drives the shame into silence.

I used casual, physical sex despite working in very public positions of responsibility. The threat of exposure was a constant worry that prevented me from ending the illicit affairs. While single, it even prevented me from pursuing relationships with women I might have wanted to date publicly. Satan's shame kept me in the silent shadows of being alone while feeding me the crumbs of meaningless physical sex.

Has your sexual compulsion met your deep-seeded desires for constant companionship, friendship or even esteem?

Brother let this be a call to action. You can be free from sexual sin. We're in this together, so I won't lead you down an empty path of back patting and good feelings. This is a treacherous journey, and one that the devil has invested heavily in. He will not let go of his grip on you because you started this challenge or said you've had enough.

In fact, that's when he's going to bombard you with more temptation, guilt and shame than ever before. Have you experienced that the more you try to escape sex's death hold, the more temptation or anxiety comes your way?

When his heat increases, you know it means his hold is

loosening. Let me tell you from experience, lots of men fold at this point. It's a scare tactic, and it works. Satan whispers that you can't leave him because if you do, he'll expose your naughty secrets and decadent acts. He hints that exposure might even cost you a job, reputation and your family. Satan likes you right where you are—afraid. Thank God, you are not alone in this.

> *Do not fear: I am with you; do not be anxious: I am your God. I will strengthen you, I will help you, I will uphold you with my victorious right hand.*
> *Isaiah 41:10*

————

CALL TO ACTION

There is only one Call To Action after this chapter, so please meditate over the question and answer no matter how much it hurts, makes you embarrassed, or you might think consequences are improbable.

1. If your sexual bondage was exposed today, write out what risks of loss you face?

DAY 2

WHAT IS SEXUAL BONDAGE?

No temptation has overtaken you except what is common to mankind. And God is faithful; he will not let you be tempted beyond what you can bear. But when you are tempted, he will also provide a way out so that you can endure it.
  1 Corinthians 10:13-14

———

Brother today is a great day to get into the details about what sexual bondage is and isn't. Also referred to as addiction, sexual bondage is a way of coping with an underlying issue. Often the issue is so deeply embedded that the sufferer doesn't even realize what the core problem is. They can only focus on the compulsive behavior and the troubles it causes.

Because I use a biblical perspective to guide you to freedom, the term bondage is possibly a better word than addiction. Unnecessary controversy stirs among the mental health crowd because the American Psychiatric Association's *Diagnostic and Statistical Manual of Mental Disorders* (DSM-5) fails to recognize sexual addiction as a disorder. Their secular view has as much to do with a slanted morality as it does legalistic definitions.

In my humble opinion, we've overused the term addiction until it has lost significance or legitimacy. Everything is a syndrome or addiction these days. Sexual addiction has become the default alibi of adultery whether it was a cause or just an excuse. Bondage is what we find ourselves in when we engage in sinful behavior and cannot or will not remove ourselves from it.

Another vital point is that sex outside of marriage is also a sin. God created sex, and it was intended to be incredibly pleasurable as the covenant seal between a husband and wife. So, as I shared earlier, when I tried to validate my own sexual activities as a single man, there was no justification at all. I was living in a sin environment, but the devil had convinced me otherwise.

What do you understand sexual addiction or bondage to be? It really includes so many variables ranging from adultery to fantasy and fetish attraction. Often sexual addiction has little to do with actual sex. It is the coping component caused by that deeper core issue.

It took decades before I understood that my acting out was connected to a dysfunctional childhood dominated by a dad who didn't allow emotion or conversation to take place in our home. Having never been told "I love you," or a kind or encouraging word spoken while growing up, I sought the affection through sex, but without the obligation of commitment or marriage.

From this point forward, let's move together in unity with

the understanding of addiction or bondage. There is a supernatural battle being waged for your very soul, and while your obsession may be the result of early life trauma or neglect, the continuing cause and behavior is sin-based and lack of spiritual healing.

———

CALL TO ACTION

1. Pray over who has caused you the hurt that led to this addictive behavior. Now, begin to forgive them. Forgiveness is an act of setting yourself free from the offender. Forgiving does not approve of what the person did to you, nor does it require you to speak forgiveness to that person. But God does want you to speak power out loud through words of forgiveness and restoration.

Sex Addicts Anonymous Assessment Survey

Do you keep secrets about your sexual behavior or romantic fantasies from those important to you? Do you lead a double life?
Yes – No

Have your desires driven you to have sex in places or with people you would not normally choose?
Yes – No

Do you need greater variety, increased frequency or more extreme sexual activities to achieve the same level of excitement or relief?
Yes – No

Does your use of pornography occupy large amounts of time and/or jeopardize your significant relationships or employment?
Yes – No

Do your relationships become distorted with sexual preoccupation? Does each new relationship have the same destructive pattern that prompted you to leave the last one?
Yes – No

Do you frequently want to get away from a partner after having sex? Do you feel remorse, shame or guilt after a sexual encounter?

Yes – No

Have your sexual practices caused you legal problems? Could your sexual practices cause you legal problems?

Yes – No

Does your pursuit of sex or sexual fantasy conflict with your moral standards or interfere with your personal spiritual journey?

Yes – No

Do your sexual activities involve coercion, violence or the threat of disease?

Yes – No

Has your sexual behavior or pursuit of sexual relationships ever left you feeling hopeless, alienated from others or suicidal?

Yes – No

Does your preoccupation with sexual fantasies cause problems in any area of your life—even when you do not act out your fantasies?

Yes – No

Do you compulsively avoid sexual activity due to fear of sex or intimacy? Does your sexual avoidance consume you mentally?

Yes – No

NOTE: If you answered Yes to one or more of these questions, you are encouraged to seek further information or help. Survey provided with permission by Sex Addicts Anonymous. PO Box 70909, Houston, Texas, 77270, World Wide Web: https://saa-recovery.org/am-i-a-sex-addict/self-assessment/

DAY 3
WHAT IS SEXUAL BONDAGE?

For God so loved the world that he gave his one and only Son, that whoever believes in him shall not perish but have eternal life. For God did not send his Son into the world to condemn the world, but to save the world through him.
John 3:16-17

———

There is a distinction I feel is important to understand when we talk about sexual bondage. What causes an addiction to sex is one topic and how it develops is another. If you look back over the course of your life as it was affected by the obsession, you can possibly retrace the path leading to where you are today. That would be the development, and we'll jump back to that after discussing the causes.

Causes of addiction can be attributed to several broad factors such as biological, psychological and social influences. These are a sample of potential causes, and are important because some, such as a genetic or chemical imbalance, are beyond our control.

Biological factors attributing to an addictive behavior include an unconventional emotional response, being impulsive, or a propensity for sensation-seeking behavior or risk-taking.

I want to share the story of Todd. Although this is not his real name, his situation is very real and may be similar to what you experience if dealing with biological factors. He had a regular job and was on the verge of divorce. His wife had confronted him about his latest affair, and he promised to be faithful.

The problem was, Todd couldn't stop the impulses without help. He said he really wanted to behave for her but when things got quiet or boring at home, his mind would begin to fantasize. His heart would begin to race, and he'd begin texting his mistress. He said the challenge to draw her back in and meet without detection excited him more each time.

Before he was able to make the rational decision to not cheat or honor the promise to his wife, he was back in the act of adultery. Todd said he knew it was wrong but the thought of getting away with it made the sex more exciting. He also confessed that thinking about hurting his wife again made him extremely depressed after the sex.

Psychological factors such as exposure to abuse or sexual content potentially contribute to hypersexual compulsion. Certain personality disorders can run parallel with sex addiction.

The majority of men trapped in sexual bondage are victims of past sexual abuse, accidental or intentional exposure to pornography as kids. The national average age for children's first experience with viewing pornography is eight years old.

Thirdly, social factors such as emotional rejection or isolation may contribute to an unhealthy understanding and pursuit of sexual satisfaction. I've shared my story, but I'll step up again for this example.

I grew up in a godless household with a dominant father who never spoke a kind word or said he loved me. As I began to retrace my life during the healing process. I realized he'd never said one kind word to me. He never physically abused his kids, but silence was his weapon to stifle sharing emotions. The result was seven kids and my parents growing up in a home where no one spoke and when confrontations arose, no one knew how to resolve them. As of the writing of this book, three of us siblings do not acknowledge four of the others. This split was a result of a lifetime of hurt feelings, anger and an inability to communicate.

The effect on me was a need for personal acceptance and validation. I found that through physical sex. It helped me feel like I was wanted and belonged. Also, from a young life of insignificance or acknowledgement, it gave me a sense of importance and control. In reality, it isolated me from legitimate relationships and locked me into an adult life of isolation from intimacy.

Modeling is also a major factor in the way we learn to engage in activities and behaviors. If your father or friends consumed pornography, for example, you may have been drawn to replicate that behavior because of your admiration for them.

Can you see how complicated sexual bondage is? It's done on purpose so that no matter what thread you tug on, Satan has the next one attached and waiting to restrain you even tighter. So, then you ask, what's the use if it's so complicated?

Brother, it's not complicated at all when we stop looking at the causes and focus only on the solution. God is the answer. His light is a healing light that will bust open the chains of bondage. We were created in His image, and He wasn't enslaved to sin.

Please take your time to read this passage from Genesis. It gets skimmed over if read at all. If you ever feel powerless or meaningless in this life, you must understand the authority God gave you from the very origin of time. I took the liberty to bold several key words to emphasize what God granted you with and what we are ordained to do.

The power of Jesus Christ is your ultimate chain breaker. You have the power through Christ's redemptive blood to break free from sexual sin. Think of this while you train for battle today. You are doing more than pursuing this challenge; you are armoring your spirit for the battle. You are not a wasted by-product of your sexual sin as the devil has led you to believe. You are God's beloved, and you are made in His very image, to be free.

*And God said, Let us make man in **our image**, after our likeness: and let them have **dominion over** the fish of the sea, and over the fowl of the air, and over the cattle, and over all the earth, and over every creeping thing that creepeth upon the earth.*

*So **God created man** in his own image, in the image of God created he him; male and female created he them*

*And **God blessed them**, and God said unto them, Be fruitful, and multiply, and replenish the earth, and subdue it: and have*

dominion over the fish of the sea, and over the fowl of the air, and over every living thing that moveth upon the earth.
    Genesis 1:26-28

———

CALL TO ACTION

1. Write out what this passage from Genesis speaks to you.
2. Write out why you feel this passage does or no longer applies in your life.

DAY 4

WHAT ARE THE SIGNS / SYMPTOMS?

"I have the right to do anything," you say—but not everything is beneficial. "I have the right to do anything"—but I will not be mastered by anything.
  1 Corinthians 6:12

————

As men, we are fixers by our very nature. We see a problem, and we charge into the fray until it's either fixed, replaced or in worse condition than ever. The problem with finding ourselves in sexual bondage is that we're often shackled by the compulsion before we realize we're in too deep.

Do you know the most common signs and symptoms of sexual bondage?

Not only is the behavior destructive, but the confusion about it adds to the stress and shame. I came from a middle-class, blue-collar home. My parents remained married until one died before the other. I graduated high school and college. I'm a pretty typical guy. Except that I had the draw toward physical sex for attention and acceptance.

Once I realized it wasn't healthy, I was powerless to stop it from happening. I wanted to be good, I just couldn't do good. That caused even more stress because now I was locked into a cycle without control over my actions. Helplessness is a dangerous feeling for men. This is where shame and guilt become compounded and we retreat into silence and secrecy.

Signs of sexual bondage come in the form of emotional, physical or both. One of the most common emotions is the fear of being alone or abandoned. It causes men to move from one relationship to another.

For another man we'll call Chuck, he wasn't good at being in a relationship, but sure hated when he went without one. Chuck said it was sort of like Tarzan swinging through the jungle. There was always a grip on one vine (relationship), and usually he confided that his hands were on more than one vine at the same time. But never would there be airtime when no vine was clung to.

Chuck said he always understood that the chances of one woman discovering the relationship with the other woman was a high probability, but he shared that he wasn't concerned about it. Chuck, like so many guys fighting the emotional struggle, didn't value women and saw them as a means for satisfying his needs.

Chuck often talked about his feelings of fear. The fear of being alone is deep rooted and requires us to dig down to discover where that fear originated. Were you abandoned either emotionally or physically as a child? Was there sexual abuse or exposure to sex in your youth that created a distorted understanding of the reality of sex being created by God for marriage?

Chuck admitted that he was sexually abused by a teacher in school. Although he thought it was cool at the time, his impression of sex had been imprinted with a negative exposure that taught him sex was dirty, and best kept in secret. The absence of emotional connection left Chuck cold and able to separate sex from caring.

There are no real physical signs of being in sexual bondage. Although there are by-products of a highly sexualized lifestyle. An inability to perform sexually is a common issue for pornography addiction. The hours spent consuming porn, and the self-stimulation until orgasm, is drastically different from the actual physical act of sexual intercourse. The irony is that the obsession with sex actually prevents you from engaging in it because you've rewired your brain's natural design. The good news is you can undo this.

The other physical symptoms of sex addiction involve the 38 percent of men and 45 percent of women who contract a venereal disease. Additionally, 70 percent of women reported at least one unwanted pregnancy that resulted because of their behavior. Sexual bondage prompts social isolation as a means of hiding your addiction and the guilt and shame of your behavior. This results in a decline in personal relationships among family, friends and work.

Brother, this is the time to truly assess where you are in your war with sexual bondage. There is zero judgment, so put the shame and guilt aside to focus on you. You are what matters at this moment in time. If you are still on the fence about whether you have sexual bondage, had sexual bondage, or may be in the process of breaking the chains of sexual bondage, check out a few more signs and symptoms associated with it.

Do you engage in:

- multiple affairs
- compulsive masturbation
- sex with strangers
- sex with prostitutes
- pornography consumption
- voyeurism
- exhibitionism

Remember, everyone approaches sex in a different manner, so no matter how slight the difference, it affects your approach to identifying the signs.

What is similar is that as the symptoms continue, so will your appetite for them. If you're not already, you will begin to surrender big chunks of your life to the sex bondage. Work usually suffers, and getting busted watching porn, having sex at work or trying to meet others to have sex with while at work will jeopardize your career.

Have you been suspected of or caught watching porn or pursuing sex while at work?

Not only does it attack your livelihood, but your ability to maintain a long-term romantic relationship decreases as you find them mundane and unfulfilling as they can never compare to the fantasy that sexual addiction traps you into. Additionally, your need to lie to cover up the cheating that occurs while you look for other people to have sex with destroys the trust and the relationship.

Now is the best opportunity to regain control of your life. We are focusing on your fight to break the chains of addiction. This demands that you come open and honest with yourself.

If not, you can look forward to a progression of your behavior until it reaches a point where you take greater risks to satisfy an unsatisfiable obsession through sex. Your desperation to feel the rush is always just a fingertip away, and you'll begin to engage in aggressive behavior that might result in your need to hurt or injure others during sex just to gain your own pleasure. This slippery slope erodes any safety net you may have relied upon and can soon lead to arrest.

———

CALL TO ACTION

If you are still in the gray about the effect or influence of sexual bondage in your life, or if you're still under the misconception that you can handle it on your own, please take a moment to write out your answers to each question. The more you answer "yes," the higher possibility you are shackled into sexual bondage.

Do you think about sex most, if not all, of the time?

Do you think your behavior is troublesome?

Is your spouse or partner concerned?

Do you feel guilty or upset about your sexual behavior?

Do you lie about your sexual behavior?

Have you tried to stop, and found you were unable to do so?

DAY 5

WHO DOES IT AFFECT?

Watch and pray so that you will not fall into temptation.
The spirit is willing, but the flesh is weak.
Matthew 26:41

———

Who would you least want to hurt in this world?

That's probably the best question to ask yourself. And now follow the question up with the reality that the person you named is exactly who you are doing the most damage to through your enslavement to sexual bondage. They may not even realize that they are being injured, but if they aren't getting 100 percent of you at your most free, then yes, they are being denied.

We carry a spirit of sin like a dark cloud. Sin separates us from God, and that opens the door for additional sin and pain. When you handcuff yourself to the devil's wrist, you, as the spiritual head of the household, expose your family to the same separation from God.

I'd mentioned that lots of guys look at sexual sin as a victimless activity, but in reality, you are the victim and so is your family. God didn't create you to live in a sin state where Satan reigns over you. The lie of it not harming anyone is just that: a lie. Satan has masterfully weaved sex throughout the history of creation to jam a gap between us and God.

You may be in too deep to even see that you've lost the relationship with Christ, but that doesn't mean He's not waiting for you. There is restoration and renewal in your life. Most importantly, there is hope for you to repair what sexual bondage destroyed. You can live the blessed life God promised.

"For I know the plans I have for you," declares the Lord, "plans to prosper you and not to harm you, plans to give you hope and a future.
Jeremiah 29:11

I also know that a spirit of defeat can jab deep hooks into your soul. So deep, in fact, that you may have adopted the martyr's syndrome. It's another tactic of the devil to keep you so downtrodden that even if handed the key to escape into the light, many struggle with placing the key in the lock and look for excuses why they can't.

Brother now think about who you love most in this world. Yes, these are the very same people who will thank you, support you and always love you. Do this for you, but never forget that they need you to do this too.

Battling sexual sin means never letting up and never

letting go of the good ground you've gained in this spiritual war.

You should feel proud of what you've accomplished by surviving even the darkest and grueling of days. Remain faithful in those moments of life when you are bored, stressed, tempted or alone with only old thoughts of temptation and lies about how satisfying sexual sin is. Actively waging war for your freedom is refusing to click on that porn URL or reply to that sexting message. Remain vigilant, Warrior.

Be on your guard; stand firm in the faith; be courageous; be strong.
1 Corinthians 16:13

———

CALL TO ACTION

1. Write out a list of people you would never want to hurt.
2. Write out a list of people you would always want to love.
3. Draw lines to connect people who appear on both lists.

DAY 6
IS THERE A CURE?

*"Our citizenship is in heaven, and from it we await a Savior, the
Lord Jesus Christ."*
   Philippians 3:20

———

Is there a cure? Only if you're willing to take your medicine!

Brother, sexual obsession that places you in bondage is not
the problem. Whatever happened to cause you to
aggressively pursue sexual sin to ease the pain is the
problem. Until you are able and willing to dig deep to reveal
what the root cause is, you'll continue to cycle through this
addiction or swing over to another form of medicating such
as alcohol or drugs.

I won't mislead you because I've got skin in this game too.
Sexual bondage can be very complex, and I've been asked
how fast can the bonds be broken. The reality of a complete

breakthrough in a set number of days is dicey and might set you up for a fall via over expectation.

It depends on many factors, but one of the most important of them is identification. Some of us know very well what happened that now causes us to rely on the sin of the flesh to get through each day, while others honestly don't know or can't recall.

Barry, a personal friend, has been unable to maintain a job and has been arrested several times for various misdemeanor crimes. His alcohol addiction has landed him in jail once for DUI. He knows exactly what started his porn addiction. One that he didn't beat until a few years ago.

When Barry was ten years old, his uncle thought he'd be the cool uncle and show his nephew naked women on a porn site. Barry admitted he was afraid and confused because he had no idea what he was looking at. But it was easy to access, it was free, and his twenty-three-year-old uncle seemed to love it. Barry said those were all the elements he needed to want to see more.

Unsupervised, Barry was free to surf the web, and with simple search entries, he found unlimited sites offering free pictures and videos. He said his curiosity soon led to obsession. As he closed himself off from family out of fear of getting caught, he also avoided friends and outside activities. The pornography made him feel special, and the more alone he became, the more the actors became his friends.

Barry said he never even knew what pornography was until he was introduced to it. He knew his brain wasn't wired to consume it, but it eventually became programmed to need the stimulation to feel pleasure.

Thanks to confessing he had a problem, his willingness to expose his darkness to the healing light of Christ and a skilled

Christian counselor to guide him through, he was able to break the chains of pornography addiction.

Secular methods of treating impulse control disorders and obsessive-compulsive disorders are regularly used when the diagnosis is sexual addiction. Treatments range from medications, and support groups to twelve-step programs. We, however, are focusing on a biblical standard for breaking free.

After decades of captivity during which I knew I was doing wrong, I just didn't know how to do right, I smashed into the reality of my past. Until then I'd never heard of past pain causing current hurts. Nor was I aware that what I was doing was medicating the actual pain I suffered as a result of that past.

Coming into a supernatural understanding of that past pain, I learned about true and complete forgiveness. I also began to talk to my wife about what my past actually was, not the façade I convinced myself it had been. I also came into a posture where I admitted there was a problem, and I wasn't able to fix it alone.

The more I had tried to "be good," or deal with it, the more ensnared I became. Have you ever tried to untangle those smartphone earbuds? The harder you tug and jerk them around, the more twisted and knotted they become. Through God-centered teaching, I surrendered my fight to Christ.

He shared the information I never had to help me understand that I was just coping and not healing. Once I understood that to heal from darkness required light, I opened up my wounds to allow God's light to chase away the darkness in my life.

I don't know how long it'll take you to read this book, but I am asking that you commit to a process of praying, accepting, identifying, confessing, forgiving and surrendering your pain to God's healing light for only 30 days. You can't pull any punches with this. It's an all-in effort.

There are so many variations when talking about sexual bondage. Pornography, prostitution, masturbation and fantasy just to name a few. While we can't tackle everything in thirty days, we sure can lay out a solid foundation for constructing a battle plan for victory.

Facing the facts is vital. Let me help take some of the pressure off of you. You're not perfect. You, just like every other human, have been born into the original sin caused by Adam and Eve's fall from grace. This isn't a license to do worse, but instead is a reassurance that God isn't mad at you, but He is waiting to receive you.

> For all have sinned and fall short of the glory of God.
> Romans 3:23

I guess this should actually be a note at the very beginning of this book, but unless you come under the spiritual authority of Christ, these scriptural principles will mean nothing to you. Have you surrendered your life to Christ and confessed your sins to Him?

This is a very real and tangible decision. It's not like a peek and see. God has the gift of eternal salvation, and it's yours for free. All you have to do is accept His Son as your Lord and Savior.

Sounds too good to be true?

Well, from a human and carnal understanding, it just might be too good. The bible is an inspired message from a supernatural God and was meant to be read and understood with supernatural understanding by His people who have accepted Him.

Receiving Christ is all about surrender. This can't be the typical macho man moment where you wave off your friends and say, "I got this." Pride prevents us guys from admitting we are weak, out of control and unable to fix the addiction. Pride trips most of us up because we're not naturally inclined to ask for help. God hates a prideful look, and He makes no bones about it.

> *Pride goeth before destruction, and an haughty spirit before a fall.*
> Proverbs 16:18

Your daily spiritual diet should also contain enough protein to sustain your daily battle plan workouts, but even more important is to include heaping doses of daily prayer. There's only one way to get to know someone, and that is through conversation. God longs to hear from you. Don't worry if you don't know what to say, or how to say it.

God wants your voice, not your vocabulary.

Consistent prayer provides an opportunity for you to confess your sins, renew your commitment to Him, praise and worship Him and ask for His help, strength and guidance in living a life in accordance to God's will.

Don't worry that you'll have to live a strict, boring life by following God's Word. There is more fun, excitement and reward imaginable in God's glory than without.

Brother, living in God's Word requires knowing God's Word. The only way to know this is to read the bible and focus on memorizing key scriptures. These will provide you with strength in your times of temptation.

I have hidden your word in my heart that I might not sin against you.
   Psalm 119:11

Becoming familiar with the Word of God will help you establish an accountability posture when it's just you and nobody is watching. But this sensation that God is watching you isn't enough at this point to beat the battle against sexual bondage.

A trusted friend or a spiritual mentor of the same sex is so valuable. They are called accountability partners. Statistically, men accomplish and usually overachieve whatever task it is they set out to do with an accountability partner. Whether it's avoiding sins of the flesh or meeting fitness goals, we always do better when someone else is there with us.

I know it's hard to open up about sexual bondage to someone. This is exactly why Satan is so successful at keeping us wrapped tight in our shame and secrecy. Opening up to another Brother who agrees to serve as your accountability partner is the best way of moving forward toward true freedom. Don't let the devil shame your game. Open up to transparency and accountability.

You should even consider sharing certain accounts with your partner, such as anything that leads you back into the traps of sexual seduction. There are various technological web-tracking tools available.

Covenant Eyes is what I used, and I gave my wife access to it so she would be alerted anytime I accessed anything or anyone that threatened my pursuit of purity. I'm not officially endorsing it, but you should seriously consider installing an accountability software to monitor all, and I mean all, of your electronic devices.

This is no time to mess around. I ask as one Brother to another Brother to be on your honor for these thirty days. There are 335 other days in the year, so all I'm asking you to commit to is a mere 30 of them.

Why 30 you ask? It usually takes three weeks of repetition before a habit becomes part of a lifestyle. Since we're not breaking a bad habit, and going deeper than a lifestyle, the 30-day commitment will help you to better appreciate the severity of the effort, and the reward of freedom that awaits you on the other side of sexual sin.

Get serious by doing what we've already talked about, and the last few things we'll cover. You are setting up defenses against the enemy's attack. And, trust me, the devil will come after you like a raging, roaring lion. What will you do? Be like Daniel.

So the king gave the order, and they brought Daniel and threw him into the lions' den. The king said to Daniel, "May your God, whom you serve continually, rescue you!"

A stone was brought and placed over the mouth of the den, and the king sealed it with his own signet ring and with the rings of his nobles, so that Daniel's situation might not be changed. Then the king returned to his palace and spent the night without eating and without any entertainment being brought to him. And he could not sleep.

At the first light of dawn, the king got up and hurried to the lions' den. When he came near the den, he called to Daniel in an anguished voice, "Daniel, servant of the living God, has your God, whom you serve continually, been able to rescue you from the lions?"

Daniel answered, "May the king live forever! My God sent his angel, and he shut the mouths of the lions. They have not hurt me, because I was found innocent in his sight. Nor have I ever done any wrong before you, Your Majesty."

The king was overjoyed and gave orders to lift Daniel out of the den. And when Daniel was lifted from the den, no wound was found on him, because he had trusted in his God.

Daniel 6:16-23

You must dig deep to overcome this temptation. Change the settings on your internet to block all pornography sites. I've been asked whether just a little porn hurts. The answer is a resounding, yes. It not just hurts; it kills the connection with God.

You've got to do everything at every moment to protect yourself from temptation. What are your triggers? If it's late nights online, then go to bed earlier. If it's a certain part of town that prostitutes frequent, take another route home. If there's a fetish that triggers fantasy and masturbation, then avoid that stimulant.

Would you walk into the enemy's encampment? No, so why play games with whatever it is that tempts you to lay your skull beneath the sole of Satan's heel?

Don't keep a stash of porn or pictures that excite you. Throw them out or delete them, or place them on the blocked setting, but do not think it is okay to keep a little something special just in case times get tough. How about a list of prophets instead a list of prostitutes? It's time to surrender everything.

Look, I've been there. I had to delete and block any woman who I'd ever slept with or had flirted with through messages. It wasn't easy because I was actually worried what they might think. Seriously, how crazy was that? My heart quickly focused on how my wife felt once I stopped thinking of poor me and began considering how she deserved so much better.

Warrior, all I ask is for thirty days. Pray, read your bible, meditate on these daily messages, stick to your personal battle plans, and protect yourself from the landmines, snares and spies that the devil has lined up. I promise that as each day goes by and you come through, you'll grow stronger and more capable of facing the next day, and the day after that, until freedom has become your way of life. You can do this in Christ.

———

CALL TO ACTION

- Write out your defense plan. What will you throw away, delete and avoid?
- Who will you delete and block from emails, phone lists, social media?
- Write the numbers from one to thirty. Reflect on how fast you wrote them and how few numbers there actually are. Now commit to sticking with me for those thirty days.

DAY 7

WHAT IF PEOPLE FIND OUT?

...just as Sodom and Gomorrah and the surrounding cities, which likewise indulged in sexual immorality and pursued unnatural desire, serve as an example by undergoing a punishment of eternal fire.

Jude 1:7

———

The age-old question of "What if?"

This is the devil's number one trick to keeping you down. That two-word sentence has led to the destruction of lives and ended the pursuit of dreams. What if I fail, what if they don't like me, what if I'm not good enough, smart enough, rich enough, and on and on and on.

What if you decided your pride wasn't as important as your freedom, or your wife or your kids, or you? If a stranger asked one hundred people about what they thought of you, what do you think they'd say? Now, in all honesty, how does what they say really matter?

You are dying inside, yet what some stranger on social media thinks about you is worth allowing the devil to keep you tethered to a leash. We've all been and will continue to be persecuted. God assures us of this.

Indeed, all who desire to live godly in Christ Jesus will be persecuted.
   2 Timothy 3:12

I'm not suggesting that we strap an old-school sandwich board over our shoulders and march downtown to announce our sin, but I ask that you consider coming clean with yourself to begin with. Next, cry out to God and confess what He already knows. If He already knows then why must we confess it? Because God wants to know your heart and that you are also aware of the condition of your own heart. Your words show where you are in the process, and whether you are willing to submit to His will and pray forgiveness of your sexual sin and receive His healing light.

Next on your list of those who must know is your wife. Data shows that in 83 percent of the time a wife suspects infidelity, their intuition is right. Make no mistake, even sexual sin without intercourse is still adultery.

You have heard that it was said, "You shall not commit adultery." But I tell you that anyone who looks at a woman lustfully has already committed adultery with her in his heart.
   Matthew 5:27-28

Some schools of thought suggest that men wait before

disclosing sexual sin to their wife until they have refrained for at least six months. I don't agree with that. Once prompted by the Holy Spirit to confess your sins, it is best to allow yourself to be moved. Keeping recovery a secret is still maintaining a secret. It's not like she's going to congratulate you for keeping her out of the loop until you worked it out on your own.

We've already talked about this, but an accountability partner is vital for ensuring your success. A brother believer, pastor, best bud, an online support resource or in-person support group are all options. Pick the one that's right for you, not the one that's most convenient for you.

THE QUESTION you should now ask is what will life be like as a free man? It will be amazing because you are free.

———

CALL TO ACTION

1. Write out your battle plan for making notifications.
2. Write out your confession to God.
3. Write out how you'll approach your wife.
4. Write out the names of three men you'd trust as accountability partners.

DAY 8

WHAT ARE THE SPIRITUAL RISKS?

For everything in the world—the lust of the flesh, the lust of the eyes, and the pride of life—comes not from the Father but from the world.

1 John 2:16

———

Satan rakes in over ninety-seven billion dollars annually through the global porn industry according to a 2015 NBC Business report. While we're focused on exposing sexual addiction, at the same time, sex is exposed to us at an overwhelming rate. It's everywhere, but it's not unbeatable. Our focus on sexual purity must be greater than the directed attacks of the enemy.

Can you name anything that has a greater effect on separating man from God than sexual sin? I'm not sure there is anything more destructive to men. If we look at the wide range of activities intertwined by sexual sin, I think we'd be safe to answer a resounding no.

I still thank God I escaped without a draw to pornography. Maybe its influence wasn't present because there was no such thing as home computers while I was growing up or even in college. I recall the 1984 magazine with then-Miss USA, Vanessa Williams. I bought the edition, looked at the pics, and with that went my first and last experience with buying, owning or possessing porn.

Unfortunately, that's not the case for millions of men. Porn is a powerful and readily available weapon used against men and women. Porn addiction is usually identified as the most prevalent form of bondage. It's easy access in the hands of almost everyone with a cell phone. Many websites offer free access, or hooks to lure us in. In 2016, 4,599 million hours of pornography were consumed at one website alone. That equals 5,246 centuries worth of watching.

By the time we're paying, we're staying.

Unless you have committed to regaining your freedom through Christ, you will find yourself ensnared in the devil's delight while your joy wastes away. The spiritual risks are simple. Sin separates you from God.

For the wages of sin is death; but the gift of God is eternal life through Jesus Christ our Lord.
    Romans 6:23

The separation from God is a spiritual death, and although God does not turn away from you, He can't look upon sin. That is why Jesus cried out to Him while hanging upon the cross, "…why have you forsaken me?"

And about the ninth hour Jesus cried with a loud voice, saying, Eli, Eli, lama sabachthani? that is to say, My God, my God, why hast thou forsaken me?
  Matthew 27:46

God the Father never abandoned His beloved Son, Jesus, but because He had taken on the sins of the world as the final atonement for sin, God could not look upon Him until the sacrifice was done. Can you imagine allowing one of your kids to suffer the most excruciating pain possible, and being unable to intercede?

The spiritual consequence of sexual sin is just that. You are creating a gap between you and the God who loves and can save you. But you must want to be saved. God will not do more for you than you want done for yourself.

Fixing this is easy. Confess and repent. BAM, you're back in good graces with God. The beauty of this is the closer you draw to God, the less you'll want to create sin environments that cause the separation. Life in Christ is not repressive or void of action and adventure. Have you read the bible lately? It's the greatest love story in the world.

Know God's love and avoid the spiritual risks of playing with the burning fire of sexual sin. When we play with fire, we're going to get burned.

For on account of a harlot a man is brought to a piece of bread; And the adulteress hunteth for the precious life.

  Can a man take fire in his bosom, And his clothes not be burned?

  Or can one walk upon hot coals, And his feet not be scorched?
  Proverbs 6:26-30

I know this seems impossible at times because every time you've gained a step forward, the devil is there to persuade you to take three steps back into the shadows. You were not always in bondage, and if you can recall those days, then use that as your anchor to pull forward into God's light.

This is a supernatural battle in the spirit realm. Christ has won the war, and you are one of His most beloved. Celebrate the victory of recovery and restoration.

———

CALL TO ACTION

1. Write out a page about what your life is like without God.
2. Write out a page about what your life is like with God.
3. Write out a comparison of those two lives and highlight the highs and lows of each.

DAY 9

ADDICTION IS NOT THE PROBLEM, IT'S A COPING MECHANISM

For this is the will of God, your sanctification: that you abstain
from sexual immorality;
  1 Thessalonians 4:3

———

We often confuse what it is that we are addicted to with being the actual problem of addiction. Alcohol, drugs and sex are not the problem. These, among many other forms of acting out, are mechanisms we turn to as a way of coping with the real issue.

Because we spend so much time, energy and money on our obsessions, we naturally remain obsessed with them, yet fail to identify why the act became necessary in the first place. Let's look at actual causes of addiction rather than the addiction itself.

Many men can trace the origin to past pain in their lives. Dysfunctional families produce sexually addicted men more than any other factor. Some data indicate that 82 percent of sex addicts report being sexually abused as a child. Whether or not abused as a child, the addicts describe one or both parents as rigid, distant and uncaring. In addition to sexual addiction, 80 percent identify a presence of addiction in their family of origin.

I justified my father's silent, rigid behavior for decades. The fact that he never said he loved me, or even said a kind word to me, never entered my mind as a cause for my draw to the flesh. We never spoke, never interacted, and not even as much as a high five for cutting the grass. Yet I made excuses by claiming he showed his love instead of speaking it. After all, he was the strong, silent type, right?

It wasn't until I sat at his bedside over the three days as he died, that I almost begged him to say he loved me. With his final breath, he took those words to the grave with him. I don't hate him for it. I try to understand his life and the tough relationship he must have had with his father.

His passing served as a permission to begin seeking the truth. It was once I understood the damage of a dysfunctional family that I accepted that my sexual bondage had always been a result of past pain. Pain so repressed that it haunted me over the course of my entire adult life, until God revealed the blessing of forgiveness and restoration.

Our brain plays an important role in our addictions. A process called neuroplasticity allows for a "rewiring" of the brain that can lead to the obsession with substances or acts as stimulation to satisfy its need. A common expression to illustrate this is, "Thoughts that fire together, wire together."

Brothers trapped in sexual compulsion don't associate it with intimacy. That's one of the many problems with it. People think sexual addiction is just being hyper-sexualized, or overly horny. On the slight exception of chemical imbalances that create a high sex drive, bondage to sex is not as simple just wanting sex or being very physical.

Whatever our original source is, the act of having sex, watching sex or fantasizing about sex does not leave us with a warm and cozy feeling. Conversely, trying to avoid unpleasant feelings or deal with outside stressors, such as work troubles or personal issues, causes more guilt, shame and remorse.

Brother take this time to open the back door to your addictive behavior and explore your past. If there are people you can speak with who may provide clues, do so, but be careful that memory and bias don't filter actual accounts. That goes the same for your memories. We sometimes become desperate for answers and allow shades of jaded recollections to fester into an untruth that creates more pain.

———

CALL TO ACTION

1. Write out your thoughts about the most common sources of sexual addiction for men. If it was family dysfunction or abuse while growing up, describe it.
2. Write out those members of your immediate family who were or are battling addictions of any kind.
3. List people who may be able to provide you with information clues about your past and incidents that may be affecting your future.

DAY 10
IDENTIFYING THE CAUSE

For from within, out of men's hearts, come evil thoughts, sexual immorality, theft, murder, adultery, greed, malice, deceit, lewdness, envy, slander, arrogance and folly.

All these evils come from inside and make a man "unclean."

Mark 7:21-23

———

I spent over twenty-five years as a cop. It was all I'd ever done and known as an adult. When I arrested a bad guy, I did what we always did. I processed him, and then returned to work to continue catching bad guys. Seems pretty simple, right?

It's basically the same once you identify the cause of your sexual bondage. Let's say you were sexually abused as a child. Now you fail to maintain healthy relationships because of the trauma and mistrust in others. So instead, you turn to anonymous sex because it allows a sense of power, control and the safety of not being wounded.

I didn't carry my arrestee around with me all day, nor did I take him home with me. I processed the arrest and freed myself from the wrongdoer. You must do the same once you capture the cause of your obsessive behavior. Process it, release yourself from it, and move forward.

The first phase in the processing is forgiveness. Whoever or whatever it was that hurt you, there must be forgiveness. It took me a while to understand the concept as God intended. Most of us balk at the idea because we see it as letting the offender off the hook for what was done to hurt you. To the contrary, forgiving someone immediately frees you from the person and the harm they caused you.

Make no mistake, God requires that we learn to forgive as He has forgiven us. God adds the caveat that if we do not forgive others, He will not forgive us of our sins. So, not only does refusing to forgive keep us shackled to our hurt and our abuser, but we remain separated from God's mercy and grace. That's no place and no way for us to live.

> Yes, if you forgive others for their sins, your Father in heaven will also forgive you for your sins.
> Matthew 6:14

I'll throw this in to help you get through the first attempts to forgive others and drop the hatred and rage you may still harbor.

You don't even have to say, "I forgive you," to the person who hurt you. You can say it in private. But God does want you to speak the words of freeing forgiveness out loud. Say it until you feel the supernatural unlocking of your spirit from the offense.

Once you forgive someone, you now have God's authority to decide how much or how little of a relationship you choose to have with that person. People think that because there is forgiveness that the relationship picks up where it was. Nope! You have the authority to slide the marker along a scale of whether or not you want them in your life.

Brother continue to pray that God reveals what caused you to launch along the path of sexual bondage. Be persistent and patient because sometimes He withholds revelations until you are in a position or have a spiritual maturity to understand or accept the dark realities.

Don't grow weary in petition. Once you receive the truths about the causes of your behavior, then begin the process of forgiving. There is incredible power and authority in "letting go."

> *...but those who hope in the Lord will renew their strength. They will soar on wings like eagles; they will run and not grow weary, they will walk and not be faint.*
> *Isaiah 40:31*

———

CALL TO ACTION

1. Write out a list of names of people who have hurt you who you must forgive.
2. Write out a list of names who you have hurt who you must ask forgiveness from.

DAY 11

You must no longer live as the Gentiles do, in the futility of their thinking. They are darkened in their understanding and separated from the life of God because of the ignorance that is in them due to the hardening of their hearts. Having lost all sensitivity, they have given themselves over to sensuality so as to indulge in every kind of impurity, with a continual lust for more.

Ephesians 4:17b-19

———

What hurt you?

I always begin with that question because asking *who* sometimes shuts us down or distorts the accuracy of the past as it conflicts with opinions about the person.

Do you know what hurt you? Was it neglect, rejection, fear, bullying, sexual, verbal, psychological abuse, something else? I know it's tough, but this is the time to press into Christ and pray for full disclosure.

As I began to recall what had damaged me, I wasn't sure what was happening or why the recollections of my past had begun to come more clearly focused. I'm not saying that it was a foggy blur, but once I started to pray and focus on exposing my darkness to the healing light of Christ, I was given a new pair of goggles.

I started to refer to them as God goggles. Things I'd done in my past and blew off as youthful indiscretions or macho shenanigans were seen differently.

Once I confessed sexual sin to my wife and focused on unpacking the causes that created a lifetime of bondage, I began to reexamine the events of my early life. Little by little God revealed what I thought were normal experiences were actually harmful actions that hurt me deeper than I could have ever imagined.

It was only because of my confession and prayers for healing that I was allowed to understand the darkness that I'd created because I was first placed in darkness. It was also because of the God goggles that I began to experience His healing light. In my conversion from darkness to light I began to understand several dynamics about sexual bondage.

While there are numerous and complex variables associated with an addictive, obsessive or compulsive behavior, I'd be willing to say that most of us men act the way we do because of past pain.

Often, the sexual sin is a search for validation. As I shared, my dad dominated the household through silence and physical intimidation. No one was allowed to discuss how they felt or show weakness. That caused rejection that haunted me almost my entire life. Of course, I didn't see it as rejection, but my spirit knew it and was deeply wounded because of it.

I spent most of my life seeking validation. From sexual conquests, to athletics, academics and career, I had an insatiable need to be acknowledged. Not for the pride or ego, but to save me from feeling so horrible about myself. I also needed to know or at least feel as if I belonged. Whether it was in a relationship, a sports team or specialized unit of law enforcement, I sought the bond of belonging to validate me.

Is this an issue for you too?

Another result of pain from trauma and abuse is using sexual sin to reclaim control. Men speak the language of respect. Often that respect is linked to a sense of being in control. Abuse, rejection or trauma strikes at who we are as men. Helplessness is our kryptonite.

Although false, sex allows us to feel like we're in charge of our own lives. Porn can be watched on demand, and searching for just the right actors, scenarios, fetishes and any number of search variables allow us to hold the power over the visual fantasy.

Soliciting prostitutes affords men a sense of control through the giving of money and demanding what sexual acts will be performed. Consensual sex also allows the man to feel as if he is in control of the who, what, when, and where. Of course, the why is because he's hurting and needs to soothe the pain.

Sex releases a powerful chemical cocktail in your body leading up to and during sex. These neurochemical rewards are addictive, and like drugs or alcohol, help us temporarily escape from the cause of our bondage.

Serotonin, dopamine and adrenaline ramp up our feelings of pleasure and create a high we begin to chase either for the euphoria or as a medication to soothe the pain. Unfortunately, like the drug addict, subsequent highs are never as high as the first one.

The best way to avoid chasing it instead of chasing your dreams, is to make the commitment today to break your chains and live free.

———

CALL TO ACTION

1. Write out how sex helps you feel validated. Exactly what does it validate?
2. Write out what caused you to chase the feeling of validation.
3. Write out how sex helps you to regain control.
4. Write out specifically when you feel you are not in control.

DAY 12

MEDICATING

You shall not covet your neighbor's house. You shall not covet your neighbor's wife, or his male or female servant, his ox or donkey, or anything that belongs to your neighbor.
Exodus 20:17

———

Brother, how do you cope with what hurts you most?

No matter how you're dealing with it right now, you are not alone. Matter of fact, some of the most heralded heroes from the bible have also suffered as a result of sexual sin. Too often we miss the full value of God's message in the bible because we automatically elevate the people to an exalted position.

The beauty in God's Word is that He uses folks just like us to do miraculous things. Not by our own ability, but by His. Let's look at David. You might recall Jesus was born of King David's lineage. He was a skilled musician and gained fame from killing Goliath. He was personally chosen by God to become king of Israel.

Unfortunately, David suffered greatly from past pain, and turned to sexual sin as a way of coping. This is called medicating. Many of us do it as a way to either make us feel better, or just not hate ourselves so much. Either way, it solves nothing about our core cause of pain.

David's pain was rooted in the rejection by his father. He wasn't considered worthy of meeting the prophet Samuel who came to anoint a ruler. Yet, there in that rejected, messed-up boy, Israel had a king. David's rejection stung and stuck. Have you been hurt by a parent, and never forgave them? This injury doesn't heal in time.

I'll share that as a kid, I'd gotten a red warm-up suit with white stripes for Christmas. It was a special gift because the track suit looked just like the one wore by my hero, Steve Austin, the Six Million Dollar Man (not the wrestler). I wore it everywhere.

One day my dad called out to me, but I was mixing it up with the neighborhood kids. Then I heard his words very clearly, "Hey, idiot in that red suit, I'm talking to you." I was about ten years old. I stuffed that tracksuit in the trash, and forty-two years later, those words still hurt.

David also endured trials as most of us do, and the eventual result was an addiction to the flesh. His most notorious affair was with another man's wife, Bathsheba. Not only did David impregnate her, but he schemed to have her husband killed in a war he fought on behalf of David.

Do you think you've messed up because of using sexual sin to medicate your hurt?

Using sex to medicate our past pains also prevents us from establishing healthy, legitimate relationships. We find ourselves asking what's wrong with us as we lose one potential relationship after another. We have a great partner, yet we can't stop cheating on her or thinking about other women. Some guys even justify this by believing their standards in women are just too high. To the contrary, they have no standards by which to realistically judge their relationship with a woman.

This is like only taking ibuprofen for cancer. You may not ache as bad, but you're doing nothing to heal. Medicating delays the healing process by allowing the root cause of your personal pain or rejection to continue below the surface. While it might not hurt as bad, it's still there doing major damage.

Here's a little more about how David's addiction. It not only affected him, but also his entire family. We've already talked about the lie that sexual bondage is a victimless sin. As David's life exposes, there are many innocent loved ones who get hurt. We'll talk about two of David's sons later, and you'll clearly see how the flesh affects more than just the consumer.

Most of us medicate. I did for years, but now is the time to stop. But the only way to stop medicating with sexual sin is to begin the healing process. Remember, Brother, only God's light can chase away the darkness of sin. You must expose your hurt to Him before that light touches your heart. Now is the time, and you've got the support of prayer warriors all around you.

You may be asking why then did God pick such a guy as David to lead His people, and become part of the family tree from which Jesus was born? God Himself chose David to be king over Israel because of what He saw on the inside. This is how God also looks at us. We're not broken or evil or irreconcilable—we're wounded. God is the great Healer.

Man looks at how someone appears on the outside.
  But I look at what is in the heart.
  1 Samuel 16:7b

———

CALL TO ACTION

1. Write out everything that you use to medicate your pain.
2. Write out how using the medication makes you feel leading up to it, during the use and immediately after.
3. Write out whether medicating has improved or impaired your life.

DAY 13

MOTIVATING

Do not lust in your heart after her beauty or let her captivate you with her eyes. For a prostitute can be had for a loaf of bread, but another man's wife preys on your very life. Can a man scoop fire into his lap without his clothes being burned?
    Proverbs 6:25-27

———

I remember walking up the three steps and onto stage. I bent forward and my professor placed the satin material across my shoulders in a doctoral ceremony called hooding. It meant I'd finally completed my academic achievement to earn a PhD. My chest swelled with pride and relief that the rigorous journey was now over.

Before I took the few steps to walk down on the other side, I began to feel that same old sense of panic, and I asked myself the question that haunted me for decades, "What's next?"

The other way I tried to cope with personal pain was through motivation, or accomplishment. I had just earned the top academic award given by universities, and the joy in the achievement lasted less than a minute. But before that night, I'd also earned a bachelor's degree and a master's degree. Neither one of those helped for long either.

When I wasn't in class, I had to crush barriers in my career by taking the most risky and dangerous assignments available. In sports, I was unable to simply enjoy the health and exercise. I had to push it past safe and sensible because I didn't find relief unless I found pain. I was like a junkie looking for my next award, recognition or promotion.

The wisest, richest and most successful human ever in the history of the world suffered from the same affliction. It was his hurt, family dysfunction, and the sexual sin of his father, King David, that drove Solomon to conquer and crush. Mostly himself.

Solomon was labeled with the curse of sexual scandal thanks to the relationship his father David had with his mother, Bathsheba while she was still married to Uriah, a noble warrior while he was away on the battlefield. Solomon's others siblings also suffered because of the generational curse of his father that continued to plague them.

Motivation and achievements were Solomon's failed attempt to soothe his pain. The more he accumulated the less he felt deserving. In Ecclesiastes 2 he shares the futility of trying to outwork his hurt.

I've included this small section of the scripture, but please read the entire chapter 2:1-24.

I denied myself nothing my eyes desired; I refused my heart no pleasure. My heart took delight in all my labor, and this was the reward for all my toil.

Yet when I surveyed all that my hands had done and what I had toiled to achieve, everything was meaningless, a chasing after the wind; nothing was gained under the sun.

Ecclesiastes 2:10-11

Do you not feel good enough, smart enough or worthy enough because of your pain and bondage? Are you working extra hours or taking extra classes or spending extra money to prove yourself worthy? It soon becomes impossible to fill these empty spaces. Our spirit requires peace, not prizes.

Brother know that there is peace in Christ. In Him is also healing and freedom from sexual bondage. We can't work our way into heaven or out of hell. Surrender instead to the love and redemption of Christ. Today is your day!

———

CALL TO ACTION

1. Write out your latest accomplishments that were fueled by a need to feel better about yourself.
2. Write out how the accomplishments actually made you feel afterward Did they satisfy your need for restoration and healing?

DAY 14
MEDITATING

Flee from sexual immorality. All other sins a man commits are outside his body, but he who sins sexually sins against his own body. Do you not know that your body is a temple of the Holy Spirit, who is in you, whom you have received from God? You are not your own; you were bought at a price. Therefore honor God with your body.
  1 Corinthians 6:18-20

———

There is a third way to cope with the cause of your pain that leads to addictive behavior and holds you in captivity. We've talked about the way King David used sex to medicate his hurts. We've also talked about Solomon's effort to outwork the hurt he suffered through motivation. Today, we'll talk about another one of David's sons, Absalom.

Absalom was also David's son and Solomon's half-brother. His pain, like many with a dominant parent, began at home. Absalom also suffered from intense guilt over doing nothing to defend his sister from a sexual attack by another half-brother.

It's not uncommon for men to become emotionally frustrated over situations at work, in their family, their health or life in general, and yet fail to say or do anything about it. It makes us feel powerless and creates internal stress and tension.

When we allow our emotions to stew until they boil into internal pain, it's called meditation. Absalom allowed the hurt in his spirit to meditate until his hatred intensified. For two years he avoided confronting his feelings and the offender before his pain erupted and he killed his brother.

Attacks against others is what often defines those of us who meditate on the hurt instead of healing it. Are you feeling the rage of regret and wrongdoings roil beneath the surface while you look for an outlet to unleash your fury upon?

When you do feel angry, please don't consider that emotion as a failure to control yourself. God gets angry, and it is an emotion that we also naturally experience. The difference is that anger is not a sin as long as you do not sin in your anger.

"In your anger do not sin":
  Do not let the sun go down while you are still angry…
  Ephesians 4:26

We've got to learn to process our feelings. It's when we bottle them up that the desire for a "release" enters our mind. Traps such as porn, fantasy or sexual sin are used to replace the act of processing the source of the anger. Of course, all this does is add guilt on top of the already raw emotions.

God placed a message on my heart that remains with me today. "Avoiding is not winning." You can only sweep so much junk under the rug. If it's confessing a wrong to a friend, spouse, coworker, or forgiving yourself for messing up once again, time does not heal all wounds. It is a lie, so don't let stuff fester in your soul.

———

CALL TO ACTION

1. Write out what incidents have hurt you, yet you've kept quiet because you wanted to keep the peace, or you just felt helpless to do anything about it.
2. Write out exactly what you would like to say and do to resolve each of the incidents you described above.

DAY 15

FORGIVENESS LEADS TO HEALING

But among you there must not be even a hint of sexual immorality, or of any kind of impurity, or of greed, because these are improper for God's holy people.
   Ephesians 5:3

———

Why are we in this situation in the first place?

I'd suggest that in about 95 percent of our cases, we were innocent as to the exposure, abuse or neglect that led us into the bondage of sexual sin. Someone else's behavior left us in this gap, and now the abnormal need for sex or porn remains while those who caused us to stumble have moved away or passed on.

It doesn't seem fair, and it's not. We're left feeling vulnerable, exposed and ashamed of the sinful behaviors we hide from the ones we love most. But what if I told you we actually had the power and authority over not only those who hurt us, but also over the pain we've been left with?

You have, and it begins with forgiving.

Forgiveness is a vital, but most often misunderstood, act. Many people, myself included, have refused to forgive others because the sense of hurt or resentment was too great. We feel as though there was too much harm to forgive. After all, why would we let the offender off the hook? So, we draw comfort while waiting for karma to get even with them. Sound familiar?

Unforgiveness causes a deficit in our spirit and the holder of the balance is the one who hurt and also holds power over our life. Anger is a destructive force, and until you learn to forgive, it will control you.

There were times when pure hatred fueled me to push forward against someone or something. But, once the issue was resolved or removed, I was left with an abandonment of who I was. My anger wasn't as much for the person's actions against me, as it was the bondage, I'd placed myself under because of their manipulation through the leash I fashioned out of hate.

Forgiveness is not about letting the offender off the hook. There are consequences for every action. Forgiving is an act of power. You are given that authority to set yourself free from the offense, and the offender.

While not biblical, the illustration is fitting. I love the quote attributed to Confucius:

"Before you embark on a journey of revenge, dig two graves."

Now, on to biblical truths about forgiveness. Do you have a verse of scripture in mind, or if you're like me and don't do well reciting them, can you Google one about forgiveness?

One of the most commonly known is Jesus' instructions

when asked by His disciples how to pray. He gave them the example of what is referred to as the Lord's Prayer. Matthew 6:9-13 includes the line, "And forgive us our debts, as we also have forgiven our debtors."

God doesn't mess around on the subject. His only Son was crucified so we might know salvation through forgiveness of our sins. Jesus Himself, hung upon a cross as they mocked and wounded Him. They laughed as they threw dice for His clothes. Instead of raging against them for revenge, Jesus exercised His power, strength and authority.

> *Jesus said, "Father, forgive them, for they do not know what they are doing." And they divided up his clothes by casting lots.*
> Luke 23:34

Allow God to show you the truth about forgiving and life-changing freedom. This is true, tangible power that you have the heavenly right to control. Forgiving also doesn't mean that you have to become friends again. Forgiving someone doesn't even require you to say it to that person.

God gives us a nugget as motivation. Matthew 6:15 says: *"But if you do not forgive others their trespasses, neither will your Father forgive you your trespasses."*

How's that for digging deep to forgive others? Talk about hate being a destructive force in your life, try living outside of God's grace. For those who still can't get past the idea that your offender will walk scot-free after you have forgiven them, here is another assurance from Romans 12:18-20:

> *Do not avenge yourselves, beloved, but leave room for God's wrath. For it is written: "Vengeance is Mine, I will repay, says the Lord.*

It won't be easy at first. It's a process of growth, so it's not meant to be easy. Try making a list to get started, of maybe the top three people who have caused you to be wounded. Maybe even include yourself in that list. Start speaking words of forgiveness. You don't have to say it to the people, but you must start by saying it out loud.

Repeat this for as many days as necessary, and I promise you will soon realize just how much hurt you've carried as caused by others. That's a lot of folks with their clutches in your life. You will also begin to know what true freedom feels like. Again, you have the power. You just have to be willing to flex a little spiritual muscle.

———

Call to Action

1. Write out a list of the ten most hurtful things that happened to you.
2. Write out a list of ten people who have hurt, harmed or harassed you.
3. Compare the two lists and link the names to the acts if it applies.
4. Every day, read those lists and say out loud that you forgive them. You don't have to talk to the person, but you must say their name out loud (in private) and that you forgive them.

DAY 16

ADMISSION / CONFESSION

Flee from sexual immorality. Every other sin a person commits is outside the body, but the sexually immoral person sins against his own body.

1 Corinthians 6:18

———

When did you first realize you had a sexual addiction? It was years before I understood anything about it. I was a single man who dated women and enjoyed sex. I never saw the harm in that. But when times arose where I wanted to commit to a monogamous relationship, I wasn't able to.

No matter how hard I wanted to be "good," I wasn't able to suppress my desire for anonymous physical pleasure. I bought into Satan's manipulation into thinking the sexual sin wasn't actually sin at all because it only involved me and another willing adult.

Never once did I consider the woman's feelings or wants. I just assumed it was always and only about sex. Sex outside of marriage is a sin, and it directly attacks you physically, mentally, spiritually, socially and psychologically. The costs are super high, and much more than we can afford.

What relationships have you lost because of your addiction? Maybe you've not fully come to terms that what you're struggling with is an addiction. It's time to face reality. It was Sun Tzu who said, *"Know thy self, know thy enemy. A thousand battles, a thousand victories."*

You've committed to this project, so even if you haven't admitted an addiction, you have high suspicions that you might. The only way you are going to shake the bonds that shackle you to the bowels of hell is to start by confessing your sexual sin.

There is no judgment among Battle Brothers. This is a book written by a man for men. Do women struggle with a similar addiction? Yes, but I have zero experience, nor was I called by God to minister to our Sisters about this affliction.

So, the questions I ask and the promptings for transparency come from a love for you and a burden I still carry as reminders of my battle for freedom.

With that said, have you taken full responsibility for your actions and understand that you are in fact dealing with a sexual addiction? If you have, congratulations and let's move toward freedom. If not, please take the time to pray and meditate over this issue.

I've included a simple self-assessment survey on the next page for reference. Take a moment to see where you stand in this battle.

I completely understand the demand for confidentiality

and will never ask you to confess anything publicly or place yourself in an environment of risks. With that being said, there is a level of transparent accountability expected in your war against sexual sin. Where that level is drawn is your call and I respect that.

———

CALL TO ACTION

1. It's vital to know yourself, as Sun Tzu said. Make a detailed list of what it is that you are addicted to. Dig deeper than just listing a broad term like porn. Be micro-specific about what type of porn you search for, or if it's fantasy-masturbation, write out what fantasies trigger arousal.
2. Read over this list and meditate about what it is that has cultivated such specific tastes. Dig deep once again to seek actions or causes from your past that moved the needle in these directions.
3. Pray over this list, and then destroy it.

DAY 17

SURRENDER

The acts of the sinful nature are obvious: sexual immorality, impurity and debauchery; idolatry and witchcraft; hatred, discord, jealousy, fits of rage, selfish ambition, dissensions, factions and envy; drunkenness, orgies, and the like. I warn you, as I did before, that those who live like this will not inherit the kingdom of God.

    Galatians 5:19-21

———

"I got this."

We guys are wired to roll up our sleeves and fix it. It doesn't really matter whether it's a space shuttle or a light bulb, our minds say we can do it. In the big scheme of things, that's not a bad way to be wired. That "can do" attitude has led to exploration and innovation throughout the history of the world.

Unfortunately, it has also left us in traps where the only

way to get out is by asking for help. Millions of men have gone to an early grave because surrender is a dirty word that will not cross their lips. Yet, there's a reason why militaries sound retreat as a signal to withdraw and reevaluate the battle plan.

On a lighter note, men didn't get the reputation for driving around lost because we were happy to stop and ask for directions. We're not going to beat ourselves up though. This is the way God designed us, and the masculine drive to accomplish has a much greater purpose than asking for directions. But like all good things it comes with a price.

We men also come with a healthy dose of stubborn pride. I'm not talking about pride in a good day's work. Unfortunately, this is the same pride God hates, or, as it's referred to in other translations, haughty eyes. When we place ourselves on a perch so that we look down upon others, or even feel we can see eye-to-eye with God, is when we set ourselves up for His wrath.

> *These six things the Lord hates,*
> *Yes, seven are an abomination to Him:*
> *A proud look,*
> *A lying tongue,*
> *Hands that shed innocent blood,*
> *A heart that devises wicked plans,*
> *Feet that are swift in running to evil,*
> *A false witness who speaks lies,*
> *And one who sows discord among brethren.*
> *Proverbs 6:16-20*

Brother, God is looking for our surrender to Him. Not so He can control us, but so the victory He has already won can be given to us. It's like winning a race but refusing to stop running for the trophy presentation. Too often, our selfish pride prevents our complete surrender. That is when we fall to temptation and the addiction of sexual bondage.

Pride goeth before destruction, and an haughty spirit before a fall.
    Proverbs 16:18

Brothers know when help is needed. It may be how to fight with more skill or run with less fatigue or love our family with no conditions. We all require the help of others. If you have a resistant spirit, please pray God will open your heart to allowing someone to help you.

In reality, by your very reading of this book, you've opened yourself up to surrender. Not to me or this book, but to the truth that you cannot break free from sexual addiction on your own. You can climb from the slippery pit of despair that Satan has dug for you, but you've gotta first grab someone's hand up.

————

CALL TO ACTION

1. Write out a description of a time when your stubbornness or pride made a situation worse.
2. Write out a description of when someone helped you in a bind.
3. Write out a description of when you helped someone else.

DAY 18

ACCOUNTABILITY

Trust in the Lord with all your heart and lean not on your own understanding; in all your ways acknowledge Him, and He will make your paths straight. Do not be wise in your own eyes; fear the Lord and shun evil. This will bring health to your body and nourishment to your bones.

Proverbs 3:5-8

———

Have you ever just not felt like going?

You've blocked out the time, cleared your calendar and to be honest, there is nothing else going on, but for whatever the reason, you do not want to go. I've been there way too many times. But then you think about the friend who said they'd meet you there, and suddenly, every one of your reasons for skipping just went out the window.

There's a psychology about not wanting to disappoint

other people. God's given us an innate desire to please others. This is why having an accountability partner is so critical in breaking free from the devil's bondage. Before you begin thinking of reasons why you don't want to use a partner, please stop and reconsider.

If I were a betting man, I'd say your first hesitation was that it's no one's business. Yes, we've already covered the issues with exposure. While I'm not suggesting you join a big support group, I do highly recommend you pray over God leading you into a one-on-one relationship with a trusted mentor.

Keeping your sin a secret is what Satan is betting on. Trusting another warrior to help keep you accountable is what God is rejoicing over. He instructs us to hold one another accountable.

> *Therefore confess your sins to each other and pray for each other so that you may be healed. The prayer of a righteous person is powerful and effective.*
> *James 5:16*

Athletes, businessmen, pastors and men from all walks of life benefit from accountability partners. This isn't someone who judges you or fusses at you when you fail. He is there to listen to you, to help you set out your goals, provide help in researching resources, and maintaining a consistent schedule of contact, or an emergency ear to hear you in times of struggle.

Proverbs 27:17 is one of my go-to guy verses from the bible. I think it says it all when talking about accountability amongst the brethren. Please take the time to pray and meditate over this simple sentence and allow it to speak to you about holding yourself accountable through another.

As iron sharpens iron, So one man sharpens another.
   Proverbs 27:17

———

CALL TO ACTION

1. Write out a list of men who you trust.
2. Write out a list of men who you admire.
3. Write out a list of men who you respect.
4. Compare all three lists. That man who made all three is your go-to guy.

DAY 19

TRANSPARENCY

Offer your bodies as living sacrifices, holy and pleasing to God —
this is your spiritual act of worship. Do not conform any longer to
the pattern of this world, but be transformed by the renewing of
your mind.

    Romans 12:1b-2a

———

Raul, a friend of mine, was struggling with an invitation to share his testimony before a group of other men from our church. The group wasn't focused on any particular area of manhood, but was a regular, small gathering of guys who prayed over each other and liked to share meals afterward.

Raul's arrival into the group was because he'd had several affairs in the few years he and his wife had been married. But now that it was his night to share testimony before the same group of Brothers who had openly shared their struggles and triumphs, my friend had cold feet.

When it came to him, Raul offered a witness-lite account of a few struggles as a kid, and how God was the focus of his marriage. I knew the look on his face was more about his fear of transparency than whether he was actually living a bible-based marriage. A few months later his wife had left him because of yet another affair.

I'm not suggesting that had Raul opened up that night, his marriage would have been saved, but the truth is, transparency was his burden. He should've first come clean with his wife. There are many ways to be transparent, but most of us refuse to do so. It took an intense conversation before I realized that I did not have a right to privacy from my wife.

The smartest thing I ever did for my marriage, and to ensure I never returned to the bondage of sexual sin, was to hand my cell phone over to her. I also gave her a list of all of my emails, social media and any accounts where there might have been information I once guarded to protect my secrets. It not only gave her the security she needed to begin the rebuilding of trust, but it allowed me to be transparent about my desire for freedom.

Failing to be transparent and open about your battle is exactly where the enemy wants us. We can try fighting in the shade, but we'll only win in the light.

———

Call to Action

1. Write out an opportunity where you can be totally transparent with someone about your sexual bondage.

2. Write out why you might be afraid of being transparent to your wife or an accountability partner.
3. Write out what you would say about your battle with sexual bondage as if you were preparing a speech for a group of Brothers.

DAY 20

COUNSELING

For it is by grace you have been saved, through faith — and this not from yourselves, it is the gift of God — not by works, so that no one can boast.

Ephesians 2:8-9

Are you open to meeting with a Christian counselor about your sexual bondage? If not, why not? Does it have anything to do with what we've already talked about regarding exposure, accountability or transparency?

Have you ever watched how a master blade-smith forges steel swords? It's an incredible process. Like God's light, a refiner's fire is involved at nearly every step. So is the pounding and pressure to extract impurities and weaknesses, along with the cooling in quenches of water.

The way of a fool is right in his own eyes,

But a wise man is he who listens to counsel.
Proverbs 12:15

Christian counselors may help you along your journey. Like the craftsman, they are experienced in seeing what the polished final product can be. They are also experienced in spotting blemishes and working through a process for removing them so they don't weaken the structure of the final product.

I'll tell you that I've never been a fan of going to see a shrink. In the early decades of my law enforcement career, we were told to suck it up. We did, and we as a cop culture ended up with crazy high rates of alcoholism, drug abuse and suicide just to mention a few issues.

As society began to better understand and appreciate the potential of sharing with a trained professional in a confidential setting, we began addressing those issues that ailed us.

My wife insisted that we work with a Christian marriage counselor after we talked about my bondage in sexual sin. While we both knew what was happening, neither of us knew why it was happening. I begrudgingly agreed to go for the sake of my marriage, but I immediately saw the benefits for revealing the why as well as the what.

Every skilled warrior goes through intensive training that not only builds their strength and ability, but also helps expose their weaknesses. A chain is only as strong as its weakest link. If it takes an unbiased third party to expose that weakness, then please consider participating.

I allowed my ego and pride to stop me from getting the help I needed for years. When I consider the damage done to myself and those I love, not considering a Christian counselor was a costly error.

Also, there is a reason I continue to specify Christian counselors versus a secular one. You are fighting a supernatural battle, and one in which the devil is heavily invested. Only a believer will understand the realms within which you are warring.

I cannot tell you how powerful it was to sit with our Christian counselor, and he allow the Holy Spirit to completely flip the script on whatever it was he'd originally intended to discuss. He was led by the Spirit of God, and spoke the words placed in his heart, not some checklist from a textbook. This is war, and God knows the value of a good counselor during those times.

For by wise guidance you will wage war, And in abundance of counselors there is victory.
Proverbs 24:6

————

CALL TO ACTION

1. Imagine you are a chain with many links. Write out a list of characteristics that make for strong links in your life's chain.
2. Now, write out a list of characteristics that make for weak links in your life's chain.
3. Write out why you do not want to work with a Christian counselor, and then compare the reasons against the reward of breaking free from sexual bondage.

DAY 21

ACCOUNTABILITY PARTNER

Therefore confess your sins to each other and pray for each other so that you may be healed. The prayer of a righteous man is powerful and effective.

James 5:16

———

We covered the topic of accountability a few sections ago, but God placed this back on my heart. I want to again talk not only about accountability, but more specifically about partners in this walk toward freedom.

Now is also a good time to answer a question I've been asked often. Can or should your wife be your accountability partner? No.

Make no mistake that your wife must be a part of the process, but she has become a victim of your sexual sin. I'm not trying to beat you up over it, but this is the time to set emotions, ego and pride aside to do whatever it takes for everyone to heal.

Expecting your beloved to manage your recovery is not the place for her. It would probably be a great time for her to seek counseling if she chooses. She is going to be a big factor in you recovering and gaining freedom, but as we discuss the role of an accountability partner, you'll better understand where these lines divide between showing accountability to your wife and being accountable to a partner.

You will most likely not share everything with your wife when it comes to lust or temptation. Therefore, you're doing a disservice to you both. Lastly, continuing to hear your slip ups, fantasies or lust usually scrapes off the scabs that she may still be trying to heal from after the initial exposure to your sexual bondage.

I do want to add that in addition to boundaries being established for protecting you from triggers leading you back, your wife must become a part of the long-term strategy going forward. This not only helps you remain focused, but it helps her begin to trust you.

Trust is built in drops but lost in buckets.
~Pastor Jimmy Evans

When she is ready, one of the avenues for your wife to participate in your daily accountability is to act as a monitor for subscriptions to online reporting software for all of your electronic devices. It's reported that about 30% of wives agree to serve in that role, so be super sensitive to her needs and tolerance levels before assuming that she would.

The best practice is to find another man to serve as your accountability partner. I know we don't like the idea, but men need to bond with other men before opening up. We aren't naturally inclined to make ourselves vulnerable, but this fight isn't in the natural realm. You're armoring up for a spiritual war, and while God leads the fight, you'll need other brothers in your corner to sustain you through the effort.

If you are going to open up, and I mean really open up about your struggles with sexual bondage, then the person you ask to be your accountability partner is crucial. We're about three-quarters of the way through this victory lap and we're still talking about coming clean about sexual sin.

It's not an easy decision. I understand. It's not even easy to be the man holding you accountable. I had a warrior reach out through Facebook to ask what was involved in serving as the mentor. We'll call him Peter. He admitted a brother believer asked him to be his accountability partner, and Peter said he panicked and said no.

Peter wasn't wrong for feeling afraid, but he was wrong for not explaining the fears to his friend. He said the guilt of failing to be there for another warrior drove him into a state of shame, but his pride prevented him from going back to the warrior in need and offering to accept that role.

I share this as a reminder of how high the stakes are in this war. Not only are we on the front lines, but everyone back at the forward operating base is being affected too. So, here are some characteristics to look for when you're making the commitment to an accountability partner:

A Christian who is mature in their walk with Christ. Unless you've become grounded in your faith, it's possible to focus on the sin instead of the sinner. Judging someone's actions is not what you're seeking in an accountability partner. Brothers who have been through the struggle are often quicker to understand your needs but may want to avoid being re-exposed to the struggles of breaking free.

An encouraging Brother helps reinforce what you are working to accomplish. They must be on your side and takes joy in your victories without giving false praise.

I know this isn't common among many men, but your accountability partner should be compassionate toward your struggles. Having someone empathize with you, or who has actually been in your shoes, goes a long way toward you building the bonds of trust and transparency.

Not everything about being an accountability partner is tender and emotional. We're men after all, and it's a good challenge that gets us amped up to meet it. I'm not suggesting a drill instructor, but hey, if that's what you need to get it in gear, then snap to attention, warrior.

We do best when offered factual critique of our behavior. It's often a hard balance between this and being critical, but we often skip over the chatter and get to the point. Facts, just the facts.

Your journey back to becoming the warrior God called you to be isn't going to be easy. It's also going to get muddy. For example, your emotions, regrets, hatred and lusts can get raw. You might even threaten or belittle your accountability partner because you see them as an obstacle between you and your fleshly desires. Your accountability partner must be emotionally stable to avoid being hurt or lashing back out at you.

Objective distance is vital for the accountability partner. It's best that your roommate or someone you see daily is not involved as you may both begin to feel cramped and reject not only the accountability partner relationship, but any other levels of friendship that may exist.

Your accountability partner must be able to see past who you currently are and into who you will become once your bonds have been broken. This means giving constructive feedback, understanding your potential for recovery and knowing when to let off the gas to give you a break when earned.

Your accountability partner is out there, warrior, now it's up to you to open your heart to the idea, pray that the Holy Spirit introduces you to him, and make the courageous commitment to ask him to help you break free.

———

CALL TO ACTION

1. Write out what you would ask your accountability partner.
2. Write out what you will share with your accountability partner.
3. Write out what you would realistically expect from your accountability partner.

DAY 22
SELF-ASSESSMENTS

Flee the evil desires of youth, and pursue righteousness, faith, love and peace, along with those who call on the Lord out of a pure heart.

  2 Timothy 2:22

———

Coming to the realization that you are trapped in sexual bondage can be embarrassing, make you angry or ashamed. It even scares us because it's a reality check into something we've hidden or denied. But reality is the only thing that will set you free from this addiction.

Many of us, and me included, prefer to self-assess any issue we may have. I'm notorious when it comes to medical issues. My doctor's title is based in academics, not medicine, but I never hesitate to avoid the medical clinic at all costs.

Once, I self-diagnosed as pinched nerve in my neck. I continued to lift weights and exercise until I couldn't hold a towel in my left hand. It turned out to be a shattered disk in my spine. Emergency surgery, a titanium replacement and a hole in the throat later, I'm still trying to guess on other aches and pains.

We need to find the balance when it comes to sexual bondage. If we go back to the beginning chapters, we've put in a lot of effort toward recognizing that we do have an issue with sexual sin. We've also worked hard to identify the cause of why we act out the way we do. Additionally, we've focused on the spiritual warfare in which we've found ourselves and worked like warriors to surrender our prideful will to God.

This is the grunt work that we warriors can do to create the gap between Satan's grasp and our way to freedom. It's also a time where we may ease up on our life's truth because the reality may sting. Right now is not the time to yank the Band-Aid halfway off. Expose yourself to you. This requires honesty and complete transparency to ensure you understand what is going on with you. No one else can want this for you more than you.

We've all heard the advice about taking a good, long look at ourselves in the mirror. It's great advice and we must do it in this situation. What do you see? Have you been completely open so far? If not, what's holding you back? What are you waiting for? Now is also as good a time as any, but please make sure you're giving yourself a fighting chance by honestly self-assessing your situation.

We fix mistakes by first understanding that a mistake has been made. Audits are the best tool used for identifying errors. Give yourself a sexual bondage audit today. What has been your compulsion? I'm going to ask you to write out a few things in today's Call to Action, but before that, it's important to pray over it.

I know this whole battle plan goes against so much of what we've been taught or observed throughout our lives. The idea of surrendering in struggle has never equaled victory, but like we've talked about before, this is a fight within the spiritual realm. God only wants our surrender so our prideful will is out of His way for our blessings.

Add the audit to your armory inventory and take a sincere look at where you are in the fight. Sun Tzu said, "It is said that if you know your enemies and know yourself, you will not be imperiled in a hundred battles…" While this isn't scriptural, it's timeless common sense.

————

Call to Action

1. Do you believe Jesus Christ is the Son of God?
2. Have you accepted Jesus as your Lord and Savior?
3. Do you believe that Satan exists?
4. Do you believe that Christ conquered death and Satan with His own death and resurrection?
5. Have you been trapped in sexual bondage?
6. Have you tried to escape your sexual bondage in the past and failed?
7. Have you suffered personally because of your sexual bondage?
8. Have you suffered professionally because of your sexual bondage?
9. Have you followed your personal battle plan?
10. How have you done daily?

11. How have you done overall?
12. Have you abstained from sexual sin?
13. Have you abstained from pornography?
14. Have you chosen an accountability partner?
15. Have you asked him?
16. If so, have you met with him?
17. If not, why not?
18. Have you kept up with the Call to Actions?
19. Are you committed to finishing this battle strong?
20. What do you see as your biggest hurdle to breaking free from sexual bondage?
21. Do you feel you will be able to overcome this hurdle?
22. If so, explain how.
23. If not, explain why.
24. Are you open to working with a Christian counselor?
25. If not, explain why.
26. Do you understand that you are indeed a mighty Warrior?

DAY 23

FAMILY SUPPORT

For the grace of God that brings salvation has appeared to all men. It teaches us to say "No" to ungodliness and worldly passions, and to live self-controlled, upright and godly lives in this present age.

Titus 2:11-12

————

Brother, is your family in this fight with you?

Way too often we go at this battle alone because we're ashamed of what we're doing or have hidden it from them and can't bring ourselves to include our family. I've also mentioned that we usually feel justified in our sexual sin because we convince ourselves it's a victimless act, but I want to show you the real damage: family.

A good man I'll call Rick, and his wife Sue, had both struggled with his sexual sin for years. He never understood

Sue's feelings of powerlessness because she didn't understand or help with his addiction. She also felt it was because she wasn't desirable enough, and instead Rick turned to other women and porn.

Sue suffered through Rick's lies and sneaky behaviors while he tried to conceal his sin. She loved him dearly, but the humiliation among their peers who knew of or participated in Rick's numerous sexual affairs became overwhelming. She was innocent, but he had broken her. Sue began experiencing symptoms of PTSD (post-traumatic stress disorder).

This loving Christian woman and mother of their three kids did nothing to deserve what Rick was doing to himself or them. Her fear of his exposure and the daily worry of him losing his job if his boss found out that Rick was consuming porn on office computers led her into a dependence on Xanax.

It wasn't until Sue began seeing a Christian counselor by herself because Rick wouldn't go, that she understood she was not responsible for Rick's addictions. Although she did learn that sex was not Rick's core problem, but that the past she knew of carried lots of personal pain for Rick.

Sue also accepted responsibility for her dependence upon Xanax but worked to break free from it. Rick on the other hand refused to address his past pain caused by a dominant father and the rejection of his parents' divorce. It was physical sex that gave him a sense of acceptance, and eventually porn that gave him a false sense of control.

The last time I spoke with Rick and Sue, he had suggested a legal separation while working on his sexual bondage. Sue admitted she'd agreed because her anxiety never decreased, and their oldest daughter was now acting out with older boys from school.

I didn't pursue the connection after that, but I learned they'd divorced, and Rick was suffering even worse than before thanks to the divorce and the job he lost after his addiction was exposed by a coworker.

It really saddened me to see where both of them and the kids had ended up. Family support is vital, and Rick had a rock-solid partner in Sue. She tried to stand with him, and even carry him when the burden got too tough, but Rick always said he was afraid of life without the comfort of his pornography. I don't agree with his decision, but I do understand the complexity of Satan's best efforts to separate us from our family and God.

If you are married, you must begin to pray for an opportunity to open up to your wife. Chances are high that she already knows and is just waiting for you to become comfortable or broken enough to talk to her. Learn to lean on those who love and support you.

———

CALL TO ACTION

1. Write out a list of family or close friends who know about your sexual bondage.
2. Write out a list of family and close friends who you've never told, but they may suspect you have a problem.
3. Write out who from the second list should be moved up to the first list and trusted with your struggle.
4. Write out ways your wife and/or family can help you through this battle.

5. Write out a list of who, besides you, benefits from your freedom.

DAY 24

CHRISTIAN SUPPORT

But sexual immorality and all impurity or covetousness must not even be named among you, as is proper among saints.
   Ephesians 5:3

———

One of the hardest things I did was to tell a close group of men from church that I had struggled with sexual bondage. I thought they saw me as this tough alpha male former cop, who rode motorcycles with them and didn't have a worry in the world. When no one was shocked at my confession, I was a little surprised and maybe even disappointed.

It wasn't a big, emotional revelation because there was no judgment. Some shared they too struggled with sexual addictions, while others offered continued fellowship. We sometimes fear fellow believers because we think they're going to judge us. If you're in a bible-believing church centered on Jesus Christ, then brokenness is something almost everyone has shared.

Ask yourself this question, "Does the devil want you with a band of Brothers, or alone in the dark of shame?"

I know the answer is simple. So, where do you think God wants you to be? Yep, in fellowship with other believers. I love what Solomon says in Ecclesiastes:

> *Though one may be overpowered, two can defend themselves. A cord of three strands is not quickly broken.*
> *Ecclesiastes 4:12*

Many years ago, I was a lieutenant running a multi-jurisdictional drug and violent crimes task force. It was a tough assignment and because of the danger, we often found ourselves with very few undercover agents to safely get the job done. I knew the risk every time we showed ourselves in public to make an arrest.

Instead of growing frustrated with a slow hiring process, I found that God laid Ecclesiastes on my heart. I printed and framed it in my office where it remained over my twelve years in that assignment. We never lost a life despite the violent scenarios that regularly played out before us. Yes, God knows we are indeed stronger together.

He created us to have fellowship. He didn't need the company, but He loved us before we were created and that is His eternal love. The way God wants to communicate with us is the way He wants us to communicate with each other. That involves close relationships where encouragement, friendship, accountability and love will be foster.

Therefore, confess your sins to one another and pray for one another, that you may be healed. The prayer of a righteous person has great power as it is working.

   James 5:16

Brother, please avoid the trap that most nonbelievers and lukewarm Christians fall into by adopting an attitude that "church people" are snooty hypocrites just waiting to judge you for having sinned. Are there crumby folks? Sure there are, but that's true in every aspect where humans gather.

The reality is that among a body of Christ-loving men, you will find the support and understanding you need to join the ranks in God's called army of warriors ready and armored up to bust open the chains of sexual slavery.

If you don't currently belong to a men's group, here's how to begin. Check to see if your church hosts small groups. Most that do will break the groups into areas of interests such as young adult, married, single, etc. Join the group that best fits you and begin building relationships with men in the group.

If your church doesn't have a men's group, offer to host one. You don't have to be a pastor or theologian to lead a group. Honestly, you don't even have to belong to a church to start your own men's group. Just be cautious that it starts with a God-centered focus and remains that way.

———

CALL TO ACTION

1. Write out the name of the church you attend regularly.

2. Write out what you like about that church.
3. If you don't attend church, write out why not.
4. Write out the names of men you know are Christians, and who you would feel comfortable asking about starting a men's group.
5. Write out what you would want to gain from a men's group, or a support group of men.

DAY 25

NETWORK SUPPORT

Put to death therefore what is earthly in you: sexual immorality,
impurity, passion, evil desire, and covetousness, which is idolatry.
   Colossians 3:5

————

While I write this section, I'm actively serving as a mentor to
a warrior engaged in a battle to break free from the chains of
pornography. We've never met, and only know each other
through my Brick Breakers Men's Ministry site. Regardless,
he's a wounded warrior who reached out for my help. We
text daily and through his honesty and openness, I've seen
more about the realities of sexual bondage than I ever saw in
my own.

I'm not saying his is worse than mine, but that we are all
victims of Satan's lie in this war for our spiritual
independence. Helping other Brothers is an opportunity to
see more of yourself through them. While winning my battle

with sexual bondage, I focused on myself and my freedom. While mentoring my warrior Brother, I see his battles from a bird's eye view. It's a sobering observation to witness the totality of consequences for pursuing his compulsion.

Networking is an important element in gaining and maintaining your freedom from sexual bondage. It's like house plans before you ever break ground. Laying a foundation that not only supports the structure and framework but will sustain against all types of stress and strain is vital for your success.

Mentors, Christian counseling, family, spouse support, technology accountability software, self-assessments, new peers if needed, proper work environment and anything that sets your stage for winning and remaining free is vital for you to overcome sexual bondage.

How do you know what you'll need? That's where mentors come into play. They've been through the battles that you're going to enter, and they've won. Nothing they tell you is theory. It's all practical experiences that share information about mistakes and victories. While mentors are a vital component of the network, you must include the other resources mentioned above and any others you identify along the way.

The truth is, you can half-heartedly stumble through a minefield and when the explosions tear at your soul, you can roll around in the muck a little longer, or you can gird your loincloth, set your armor and claim the victory over Satan's prize tactic: sexual bondage. This Armor of God verse is encouraging, so please take the time to pray and meditate over it.

Finally, be strong in the Lord and in his mighty power. Put on the full armor of God, so that you can take your stand against the devil's schemes. For our struggle is not against flesh and blood, but against the rulers, against the authorities, against the powers of this dark world and against the spiritual forces of evil in the heavenly realms.

Therefore put on the full armor of God, so that when the day of evil comes, you may be able to stand your ground, and after you have done everything, to stand.

Stand firm then, with the belt of truth buckled around your waist, with the breastplate of righteousness in place, and with your feet fitted with the readiness that comes from the gospel of peace.

In addition to all this, take up the shield of faith, with which you can extinguish all the flaming arrows of the evil one.

Take the helmet of salvation and the sword of the Spirit, which is the word of God.

Ephesians 6:10-20

———

CALL TO ACTION

1. Write out what your network requirements (resources) are to break free of sexual bondage.
2. Write out what your network requirements (resources) are to remain free of sexual bondage.
3. Write out what you would say to explain your sexual bondage to your mentor.
4. Write out how it makes you feel having to share your story with another man.
5. Write out what remaining free means to you.

DAY 26

TASTE OF FREEDOM

For this is the will of God, your sanctification: that you abstain from sexual immorality.
    1 Thessalonians 4:3

I want to share a story of success so that you may know it is both possible, and yours to claim. Carl was another warrior who came to me for help with his sexual bondage. It had consumed all of his adult life, and at forty-three years old, he didn't see the possibility or the use of trying anymore.

Who doesn't love a good war story where the good guy wins! I'm going to give you a spoiler alert just in case, but Carl wins the fight. Sorry, I just couldn't resist. But he put in the work and came out on top. These are a few of his milestones that got him there and keep him there.

We cannot fight lust with our flesh. It's a spiritual battle that's out of our control. Once we accept that and understand the desperate nature of our position, we come closer to God and His saving grace. Carl also came to understand that he had to drop his miserable attempts at deception.

While he thought he'd become pretty good at covering his tracks, the truth was he was an embarrassment to himself and his family. He confessed to justifying his struggles with porn on occasions by claiming it wasn't that harmful and helped him relieve stress. It was more deception and he finally made the choice that there could be no place in God's grace for porn.

Carl came to know that the more he closed himself off from his family, the more he felt the cruel desire for lust. Satan wants to isolate you from supportive people who love you. He wins once you trust him to give you validation through sexual bondage and pornography. Hiding our sins only enforces them. Confession frees you from them.

Carl, and most of us are doers and fixers. Relying on others is a sign of weakness. But, in the supernatural realm of sexual bondage, relying on God's strength was Carl's only option to find and maintain freedom. Only by surrendering his fantasy and carnal thoughts to Christ was he able to establish and uphold a holy standard of sexual purity.

Carl was blessed with a taste of freedom, and while he basked in Christ's light, he committed to remain free. While God set him free, Carl knew he had to remain on guard against his own pride.

Be alert and of sober mind. Your enemy the devil prowls around like a roaring lion looking for someone to devour.
   1 Peter 5:8

Warrior, the keys to Carl's success are that he remained

humble about his victory. He knew the dangers of pride, so he remained close to Christ. He consistently pursued the Holy Spirit for guidance, was obedient to His prompting, made sure he didn't squirrel himself into situations of being alone or isolated, and made sure he stayed active in small groups at church or service projects where service to others was placed above sexual satisfaction of self.

GOD ALLOWS us glimpses of brilliance to stir our spiritual imagination and encourage us to pursue His wonderful will for our lives. Once you experience a taste of freedom, it should be hard to return to the bondage. But I know that in reality that although the shackles have been removed, it may be harder to flee than expected.

The mighty elephant, once subdued, remains tethered by a mere rope around its leg attached to a small peg in the ground. It's only the perception of bondage that we struggle with, because the reality is, we were set free when Jesus went to the cross. Enjoy everlasting freedom from sexual bondage.

―――

CALL TO ACTION

1. Write out in as much detail as possible the last memories you have of freedom before you were subdued by sexual sin.
2. Write out in as much detail as possible the most recent taste of freedom from the chains of sexual sin.
3. Write out in as much detail as possible what you envision complete freedom from sexual sin will be like.

DAY 27

PERSONAL COMMITMENT

You shall not commit adultery.
Exodus 20:14

———

Brother, are you living a life outside God's spiritual ABCs: Accountability, Boundaries and Consequences? It's time to make a lasting personal commitment to reclaiming your life. These three simple principles can and will change your life. But you must be willing to actively participate in gaining and maintaining your freedom.

Have you ever wondered why your life continues to be one struggle after the next? No matter how hard or bad you want to change, you don't. It's true that the path to hell is paved with good intentions. Intending to do something like break free from sexual bondage doesn't bring healing or change. It only brings more hurt and failure. The true healing comes when intentions stop, and actions begin.

We're naturally resistant to limitations. We like to explore, push and look beyond. While these can be great characteristics for innovations and improvements throughout history, they have also caused us great problems when we either didn't know where the limits were, or we just refused to stop.

Resistance to standards and aggression to conquer cannot be what solely drives our life. Everyone needs structure. If we want true, eternal life-winning change, we need to be accountable, respect established boundaries and understand that there are serious consequences to our actions. My pastor, Joshua Melancon, once told me, "God isn't going to wink at your indiscretions anymore."

That simple sentence pierced my spirit. I'd always assumed God would forgive me because I was a good guy. There comes a point where being a good guy and having good intentions doesn't cut it.

Brother, please take time to pray about these ABCs, and if you truly want to stop asking, "Why me?" and start living a strong, active life for Christ that's free of the shame of sexual sin, then put them into practice.

Remember, fences are built to protect what's on the inside, and not to limit how much you can achieve in this life. Don't hesitate to construct the boundaries that protect you from porn and sexual invasions.

CALL TO ACTION

1. Write out a list of tactics you have or that you will put in place to hold yourself accountable.

2. Write out a list of boundaries you have or that you will put in place to protect yourself.
3. Write out a list of consequences you have, will or may face for continuing to serve Satan's desire through sexual sin.

DAY 28
HOLDING ONTO FREEDOM

The body is not meant for sexual immorality, but for the Lord, and the Lord for the body. By His power God raised the Lord from the dead, and He will raise us also. Do you not know that your bodies are members of Christ Himself? Shall I then take the members of Christ and unite them with a prostitute? Never!
   1 Corinthians 6:13b-15

———

Brother, if you've experienced just a taste of what freedom from sexual sin feels like, then I know your heart must yearn for the security of living a consistent life of liberation. Maybe you've escaped for a few days, weeks, months or even years before being reclaimed by the unrelenting lures of sexual bondage. The binge-purge cycle is vicious but is a favorite tool of the devil's trade to spin you deeper beneath the surface.

I'm originally from the bayous of south Louisiana. Matter

of fact there is a very popular show about alligator hunters based around the parish I grew up in. The reason I bring this up is because that's the tangible image God puts on my heart while I pray for your freedom.

It's called the death roll, and is what alligators use to kill their prey. It's fast, violent and immediately disorienting to the victim. Once that old gator begins to roll, there's little chance you'll resurface. If you are the few who have, it won't be unscathed by missing limbs or disfiguring scars.

If we play at the edge of murky waters instead of standing firm on the solid ground like God wants, we place ourselves at risk. Gators are masters of stealth in the water. Not so much on solid ground.

If you want to hold onto that sweet taste of freedom, then where do you suppose you should be? Too many men think they can dance between the shoreline and the solid ground and have it both ways.

That is a lie. You do know who the father of lies is, don't you? In that case, stop playing with your eternal freedom. You can live the good life by grasping onto freedom from sexual sin. It's one moment at a time.

It's sitting at the computer with the porn site search listed on screen and calling out to God. He'll deliver you from the session of consumption. Learn to listen to the Holy Spirit when you're being led away from the barrooms or to delete the mistress's phone number and hookup text messages.

It's not easy.

God knows it's not easy.

But through Him, all things are possible, and in time, God will remove the desire for sexual sin from your heart. You may ask why He doesn't just take it away without you having to struggle, and I'll remind you that God loves us so much that He gave us free will. Otherwise, we'd be mindlessly chewing cud with the cows. You are so much more than the sum of your mistakes. You are a child of God.

> *But Jesus looked at them and said to them, "With men this is impossible, but with God all things are possible."*
> *Matthew 19:26*

———

CALL TO ACTION

1. Write out a story showing what it is like to grasp onto freedom. Be sure to include all of the senses when describing your victory. Sight, sound, smell, touch and taste.
2. Write out exactly how you'd describe your freedom from sexual bondage to another warrior in the fight.

DAY 29

SPIRITUAL COMMITMENT

My son, give me your heart and let your eyes delight in my ways, for an adulterous woman is a deep pit, and a wayward wife is a narrow well. Like a bandit she lies in wait and multiplies the unfaithful among men.

Proverbs 23:26-28

———

We've come a long way together. Your mind, body and spirit have had the chance to become completely overhauled. Are you where you thought you'd be before you started? Any forward progress is advancement, so be proud of what you've accomplished. I am grunting with pride for you.

The most important change during this freedom fight must be your spiritual fitness. All of the muscles in the world won't stop the tiniest of darts that the devil will launch your way. Sure, physical training is vital to take control over your body and to demonstrate your ability and willingness to be obedient, but spiritual fitness will snap the chains of oppression right off.

> *...but those who hope in the Lord will renew their strength. They will soar on wings like eagles; they will run and not grow weary, they will walk and not be faint.*
> *Isaiah 40:31*

Just like exercising the body daily improves your strength, consistent prayer makes you spiritually strong. The more we make us less about us and more about Christ, the easier it is for us to remain free from sex's lure back to slavery.

Praying through temptation, and while giving praise, not only connects directly into the Holy Spirit pipeline, but keeps humility at the forefront of your restoration.

You know that sin separates us from God. As a matter of fact, the bible doesn't mince words when referring to sin. The wages are death.

While committing sinful acts may result in your physical death, the context in Romans 6:23 is a spiritual death because of the separation from God. Can spiritual life be restored? Yes, it can. Confession, repenting and living a life in pursuit of Christ will redeem and restore you to His grace.

> *For the wages of sin is death; but the gift of God is eternal life through Jesus Christ our Lord.*
> *Romans 6:23*

Brother, please don't fall back into the sexual snare by pounding your chest for your most recent victories. Build a strong relationship with the Holy Spirit so you'll have God's helper to steer you clear of the minefield.

Your depth of spiritual commitment will determine your success at breaking and staying away from sexual sin. You're in a spiritual war and need supernatural weapons. The Holy Spirit will armor you for victory. Pursue Him.

If you love me, you will obey my commandments. I will ask the Father, and he will give you another helper who will be with you forever. That helper is the Spirit of Truth. The world cannot accept him, because it doesn't see or know him. You know him, because he lives with you and will be in you.
John 14:15-17

———

CALL TO ACTION

1. Give glory to God.
2. Write out a thank you letter to God for giving you this victory.
3. Write out a letter to yourself and don't look at it for at least three months. Tell yourself how you feel at the moment of writing the letter. What you have accomplished and, although tough, just how satisfying walking in freedom feels.

DAY 30

WALKING IN FREEDOM

For all have sinned and fall short of the glory of God, and are justified freely by his grace through the redemption that came by Christ Jesus.

Romans 3:23

———

Brother, I had written this great word for you to meditate upon for today. In my mind it was the scene similar to the movie *Braveheart* when William Wallace paced his steed back and forth before the warriors and emboldened their fighting spirits with his words of duty, honor and sacrifice.

But the truth is, you are a warrior and move to the beat of your own drum. Maybe it's a rebel yell that fires you up to keep temptation at bay, or it's a careful thought about the consequences of failure that motivates you. I respect you for your effort and your desires to know eternal freedom through God's victory.

Let the ancient Hebrew war cry, *Rak Chazak Amats*, stir your soul and strengthen you in the midst of temptation. When you've fallen down and hesitate to stand right back up, allow these words to resonate in your spirit, and know that the mighty God on high loves you, cherishes you and waits upon you to claim the victory.

His only Son went to the cross so you may live the life God intended you to live. Not as a slave to the deceiver and father of lies, but as a child of God and a son of the kingdom. You have been wounded, but you have not been defeated.

"For I know the plans I have for you," declares the Lord, "plans to prosper you and not to harm you, plans to give you hope and a future.
   Jeremiah 29:11

Jeremiah's words are not a eulogy, but a victory speech. You've come so far over the course of this challenge, but in reality, it wasn't a challenge. It was simply a way for you to clear the dust and see the shine of the King's crown that He had for you.

Allow these words to live in your heart and be fueled by scripture and prayer. *Rak Chazak Amats* means all strength and courage for the glory of our God, while rushing headlong into the most hazardous and impossible battles without pausing to consider the possibility of defeat.

This is how you bust open the gates of hell's sexual bondage lies and grasp onto freedom in Jesus Christ. This is also how you remain a free man. Forever gone are the days of isolation, guilt, shame and the fear of the devil's blackmail. You are a new creation in Christ, so claim it and live it. No turning back, Brother. No turning back.

God bless you,
Your Brother in Christ,
Scott

MOVING FORWARD

THE CONQUERING STRONGHOLDS STUDY & LEADER GUIDE

Congratulations on having the courage and the humility of a teachable spirit to meet me here. It's not easy and is probably why it took me so long to come here also. In Christ, what matters is not where we've been, but where we are going.

Let's agree to settle for nothing short of complete freedom from sexual sin. Don't let anything else in this life interfere with reaching our goal.

I want to encourage you to check out the companions to this challenge. The Conquering Strongholds Study Guide and the Leader Guide are a 10 session discussion guide to help you apply what we've covered in here. This is your personal journal of success, so if you sandbag it, you're only cheating yourself.

Well, let me correct what I just said. We're in this together, so not only will you let yourself down, but everyone else who truly cares about you will be disappointed. But because we love you, we will not abandon you.

Make the most of the opportunity that has been given to you.

Welcome to Freedom,
Scott

DR. SCOTT SILVERII

Dr. Scott Silverii is a son of the Living God. Thankful for the gift of his wife, Leah, they share seven kids, a French bulldog named Bacon and a micro-mini Goldendoodle named Biscuit.

A highly decorated, twenty-five-year law enforcement career promptly ended in retirement when God called Scott out of public service and into HIS service. The "Chief" admits that leading people to Christ is more exciting than the twelve years he spent undercover, sixteen years in SWAT, and five years as chief of police combined.

Scott has earned post-doctoral hours in a Doctor of Ministry degree in addition to a Master of Public Administration and a Ph.D. in Cultural Anthropology. Education and experience allow for a deeper understanding in ministering to the wounded, as he worked to break free from his own past pain and abuse.

In 2016, Scott was led to plant a church. Exclusive to online ministry, Five Stones Church.Online was born out of the calling to combat the negative influences reigning over social media. Scott's alpha manhood model for heroes is defined by, "Be on your guard; stand firm in the faith; be courageous; be strong. Do everything in love." (1 Corinthians 16:13-14)

ACKNOWLEDGMENTS

I give all glory and praise to my heavenly Father. It was His son, Jesus Christ who lifted me up when I wanted to stay down, and the Holy Spirit who now pours life into my soul so that I may pour out into others.

I want to thank my loving *ezer*, Leah and our wonderfully blended family of kids and a French Bulldog, Bacon and Micromini Goldendoodle, Biscuit. He's tiny but tough.

A special appreciation to my editor, Imogen Howson, and cover artist Darlene Albert of Wicked Smart Design.

PAYING IT FORWARD

- Watch out for your other Brothers in need.
- Share Conquering Strongholds with other men.
- Leave a review online wherever you bought this book.
- Start a men's group to help other Brothers find their way out of the darkness.
- Message me for interviews, speaking, blog tour or questions. personal email - scottsilverii@gmail.com
- Be the Man that God created you to be!

ALSO BY DR. SCOTT SILVERII

Favored Not Forgotten: Embrace the Season, Thrive in Obscurity, Activate Your Purpose

Unbreakable: From Past Pain To Future Glory

Retrain Your Brain - Using Biblical Meditation To Purify Toxic Thoughts

God Made Man - Discovering Your Purpose and Living an Intentional Life

Captive No More - Freedom From Your Past of Pain, Shame and Guilt

Broken and Blue: A Policeman's Guide To Health, Hope, and Healing

Life After Divorce: Finding Light In Life's Darkest Season

Police Organization and Culture: Navigating Law Enforcement in Today's Hostile Environment

The ABCs of Marriage: Devotional and Coloring Book

Love's Letters (A Collection of Timeless Relationship Advice from Today's Hottest Marriage Experts)

A First Responder Devotional

40 Days to a Better Firefighter Marriage

40 Days to a Better Military Marriage

40 Days to a Better Corrections Officer Marriage

40 Days to a Better 911 Dispatcher Marriage

40 Days to a Better EMT Marriage

40 Days to a Better Police Marriage

More titles from
Five Stones Press

fivestonespress.org

Made in the USA
Monee, IL
19 March 2023

30175008R10095